Took's Eye View

Also by Barry Took

FLOOK AND THE PEASANTS' REVOLT
(with Trog)
THE BONA BOOK OF JULIAN AND SANDY
(with Marty Feldman)
THE MAX MILLER BLUE BOOK
LAUGHTER IN THE AIR
An informal history of British radio comedy

Took's Eye View

Views, Reviews and Reflections

by
Barry Took

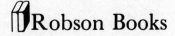
Robson Books

For Eileen and Rafe

Acknowledgements
I would like to thank the Proprietors and Editors of the magazines in which some of these pieces originally appeared, and particularly Bryn Frank, the Editor of the British Travel Authority magazine *In Britain*; Nicholas Gordon of the *Daily Mail*; Alan Coren, the Editor of *Punch*; Brian Gearing, the Editor of *Radio Times*; Edward Durham Taylor, the Editor of *Television Today*, and William Davis, the Editor of *High Life*. Thanks also to Stella Richman for permission to recycle How Not To Write A Screenplay, and to Cockburn Smithes and Co. for permission to use the S. J. Perelman anecdote which I first wrote as an advertisement for Cockburn's Special Reserve Port.

FIRST PUBLISHED IN GREAT BRITAIN IN 1983
BY ROBSON BOOKS LTD., BOLSOVER HOUSE, 5-6 CLIPSTONE STREET, LONDON W1P 7EB. COPYRIGHT © 1983 BARRY TOOK.

British Library Cataloguing in Publication Data

Took, Barry
I. Title
082   PR6070.0/

ISBN 0-86051-246-0

Phototypesetting by Georgia Origination, Liverpool
Printed in Great Britain by Biddles Ltd, Guildford.

Contents

Introduction

In the last twelve years or so hardly a week has gone by without my writing something either for a newspaper or magazine. I've written for *The Times* and for *Titbits*, a magazine boosting the wares of Sony and a Church of England parish magazine. I've written for *Punch* a great deal, the *Daily Mail* slightly less, and occasionally for anyone who has asked.

The curious thing is that I am only by accident a journalist at all. I am by profession a radio and television script writer, which is a very different business. There it's the invention of characters and the way that those new-minted phantoms speak that is important.

In writing for the printed page it's a question of presenting a mixture of fact and anecdote in such a way that the facts don't become dull in recounting them and the anecdotes don't sound wearily dragged in for the occasion. The aim of the writer of prose is to engage the *mind* of the reader; with radio and television the first consideration is the emotional response.

It was Miles Kington and Alan Coren, at that time (1971) Literary Editor and Deputy Editor of *Punch* respectively, who were principally responsible for my writing regularly, for although I'd had articles published in the *Radio Times*, *TV Times* and *The Listener* before then, they encouraged me. I value their patronage. The Editor of *Punch* at that time was William Davis, and it was he who asked me to become the deputy to their then theatre critic, Jeremy

Kingston, and subsequently to become a full-blown film critic in my own right. My association with Bill Davis diminished somewhat when he left *Punch* to concentrate on his airline magazine publishing empire, but I stayed on as film critic when Alan Coren became Editor, and wrote a weekly column until a sense of wasted time and deep frustration overtook me, and I resigned.

I had lost the taste for sitting in the dark for hours on end and then trying to write cogently about wretchedly inadequate stories constructed by complete strangers eight thousand miles away and four years before. In short, I quit the movies and concentrated on my television work.

I was heavily engaged at that time in the BBC's Adult Literacy Project, 'On The Move' (the one with Bob Hoskins in it) and couldn't really spare the two days of solid cinemagoing that the critic's job entailed. Working for *In Britain*, a magazine promoting the attractions of these islands, has a similar inhibiting factor in that it is only rarely that I can afford to spend the three or four days required to visit the places to be written about and observe them with any degree of accuracy.

My early work in the theatre was solo and in doses of a week at a time, and since then I have tended to cut and run when I become bored. So it has been with journalism. The thought of being tied to a paper or a magazine for years on end chills my blood, but one benefit that writing brings is that it keeps you in touch with reality. An actor can become vain, overbearing and immodest. No writer can afford these luxuries. It is humiliating to have an article rejected or to be told, 'We don't like the last three paragraphs. Will you rewrite them by tomorrow,' and it's not that much fun to be told, as one editor has told me on more than one occasion, 'It's amazing how much better your stuff reads when it's actually in the magazine.'

But I suppose you get used to anything and writing reviews or features certainly sharpens up your responses and makes you more able . . . for what, I wonder? To write another article, I suppose.

Anyway, this book is a fair representation of what I've seen and how I've felt, and with any luck it will harmonize with your experience. If it does that I shall be delighted.

B.T.

8

Part One

Views

The Music Hall

My family had no connection with show business whatever. My father could, on occasions, be uproariously funny but the occasions became fewer as ill health and business worries crowded in on him as he 'went up in the world' of wholesale grocery. His background was South London working class and he retained, and I inherited, a taste for the rough and tumble of the music halls. It was a family treat in the late 1930s to go to Finsbury Park Empire or Wood Green Empire and I subsequently worked at the latter as stage hand, then later as comedian, and later still, when it had become a television studio, as (briefly) the star of my own series.

In my time on the halls I travelled all over the British Isles from Folkestone to Belfast and from Llanelly to Glasgow. There were weeks when I didn't get a laugh and weeks when I stopped the show. I made friends and I learned independence and thrift – when you're earning £17.50 a week less 10 per cent commission you can't avoid being thrifty.

Those days are dead and gone for ever. The music halls flourished for a hundred years and then vanished almost overnight. I wonder if television will last as long?

When Noel Coward heard the news that Gertrude Lawrence was to appear in her first 'serious' play, *Susan and God*, he sent her a telegram reading: 'Legitimate at last — won't Mother be pleased.'

The gulf between the legitimate and the rest of the theatre was, until quite recently, virtually uncrossable. Today, when it's almost obligatory for stars of musicals to be unable to sing, the gap isn't quite so big, but even twenty-five years ago the distance between serious theatre and music hall could best be measured in light years.

S. J. Perelman writes grittily but nostalgically of his youth in Providence, Rhode Island and the time he first saw the Marx Brothers on stage. The supporting attractions, he remembers, were 'Fink's Trained Mules, Willie West and McGinty in their deathless house-building routine, Lieutenant Gitz-Rice declaiming Mandalay through a pharynx swollen with emotion and coryza, and that liveliest of nightingales, Grace Larue.'

As with Perelman in Providence in 1916, so with me in Wood Green in the 1940s. It wasn't long before I became hooked on comedians — Max Miller, Wheeler and Wilson, Vic Oliver, Arthur Askey, Syd and Max Harrison, and the great Sid Field. It was only a matter of time, application, and the shrewd theft of other people's jokes before I found myself (in 1951) actually *in* show business as a stand-up comedian 'on the halls'. Someone has defined the romance of the theatre as being in a state where even though you know the horrors, miseries and discomforts of life backstage you still feel a sense of excitement when you walk through the stage door. It wasn't long before the horrors of touring as a variety 'turn' became apparent.

Theatrical 'digs' could be pleasant, homely places, but could also be hell. At one place I stayed I was kept awake by rats gnawing at the floorboards. I've spent the worst part of a week in a room so dirty that the RSPCA would have prosecuted if an animal had been kept there. I've stayed in digs where the landlady's concept of catering revolved entirely around what the local fish shop was frying that night. But every coin has its other side. I remember Glasgow and Edinburgh with love and affection for the sweet-tempered landladies and the superb traditional Scottish food. Blackburn for the landlady who seeing me on stage and supposing, wrongly, that my act was sophisticated, served me coffee instead of tea for the rest of the week — Nescafé being her concept of the ultimate in sophistication.

Touring the provinces as part of a music hall bill is a different kettle of rock salmon from touring with a straight play. With the play, especially if it's being tried out prior to opening in London, the days are spent rehearsing, discussing the problems of interpretation and matinées. With twice-nightly variety, each performer had his, her or their set routine and once the Monday morning band call (the music rehearsal with the orchestra) was completed, the rest of the week, apart from the moments of actual performance, was as empty as a freshly-dug grave. One was rarely in the town from choice and seldom, if ever, had friends or relatives to visit. Furthermore, you were only there for a week and unlike the actors in the local repertory companies who could set up home for the season, there wasn't time to put down roots.

Ninety-nine times out of a hundred, furthermore, you were a foreigner with no local affiliations whatever. The obvious time-fillers, the cinema, the billiard hall and the pub, were usually available, but pubs close at half-past two, and even the enchantment of billiards played with bent cues on lopsided tables wears off after a time.

It was in Manchester that the lightning, as it were, first struck. I was wandering round the town one rainy day, broke, lonely and miserable, when I found myself outside the art gallery. I thought, well it's dry in there, probably warm and it's certainly free. So I went in. It wasn't that I didn't like paintings and sculpture and it wasn't that I was ignorant of art galleries, having gone often to the National Gallery in London, but curiously I felt *shy*. After all it wasn't *my* town, it wasn't *my* gallery and at twenty-three I was still far from sure of myself, but gritting my teeth a bit, in I went.

The first thing I saw — or rather the first thing I now remember seeing — was Rodin's statue, 'Age of Bronze'. It wasn't the original, as I subsequently discovered, but a reproduction — although it was none the worse for that. It stood in the centre of a cool, high room and the figure looked as if it would be warm to the touch. I *did* touch it and it wasn't. But the small explosion in me on seeing the statue still reverberates through my system. Years later on honeymoon in Paris, my wife and I visited the Rodin Museum every day — just for a gawp, as it were, but nothing ever repeated the awakening realization of the greatness of art as did that first face-to-face meeting with Rodin's 'The Age of Bronze' in Manchester in the early 1950s. From that first jolt into awareness it was a short step to

13

regular visits to the art gallery of whatever town I visited.

Stockport had, and I assume still has, a small but perfect L. S. Lowry. In Glasgow I saw, and remember with awe, Salvador Dali's 'Christ on the Cross of St John' on loan for a special exhibition. Lincoln has more excellent Lowry's. Liverpool's Walker Gallery boasts, if not the best, then certainly the biggest, pictures in England. Of course they also have excellent modern exhibitions. Once when I was in there staring open-mouthed at 'When did you last see your father' I felt the prod of an umbrella in my back. The umbrella was being wielded by a charming little old lady who, getting my attention, asked sweetly if the room we were in was the one that housed the 'contemporary Scottish watercolours'. I couldn't resist the impulse to tell her that it was. She thanked me and I left her peering through her lorgnettes at the acres of well meaning nineteenth-century English oil paint that dominated the room. I know I shouldn't have done it, but that umbrella was *sharp*.

Preston offers Singer Sergeants in profusion. Harrogate and Bath, while offering all kinds of delights, present *themselves* as the *pièce de resistance* as if to say 'look, aren't we beautiful' — and indeed they are.

But there's more to spas than their architecture or their Roman remains, and not all the pleasures of my provincial touring days were indoor ones. The thing Londoners forget about being out of town is how near you are to the countryside. However bleak and industrial the centre of the town may be, fields and hills are never far away. The Brontës' house and museum at Haworth is only a short car ride from Halifax, Keighley and Bradford. It also has some excellent pubs (one of them has a ghost) and a smashing open-air railway museum. It's not unlike the Transport Museum near the Warner Studios in Burbank, California, except for the smog. That's to say there isn't any in Haworth.

Not that I'm saying that the weather can't be frightful up there on the moors, but in summer walking up, down or around the Pennines you feel a sense of freedom and escape that's rare in the modern urban world. J. B. Priestley writes with great understanding of that part of the world, especially in his book *Lost Empires*, which is, coincidentally, about the Music Halls. But Priestley was born in Yorkshire and has a special view of it. For me, London born and bred, the Yorkshire towns were at first a moonscape, unknown and alarming. As I got to know them, York, Leeds, Huddersfield, Sheffield, Rotherham, Wakefield, Hull,

Middlesbrough and the rest, I became aware that Yorkshire — like a homespun Texas — thinks a lot of itself, is self-sufficient but is happy to share with a stranger. They've got a lot to share. The coast from Spurn Head to Whitby is glorious and the beauties of York Minster, the splendid race tracks of Beverley, Doncaster, Ripon and the rest, Leeds with its tradition of fine music, good restaurants and better hotels need no plug from me.

In my variety days I didn't aspire to hotels of any class, and took pot luck with my fellow 'illegitimates' in whatever theatrical boarding houses had a room for the week, and working in any theatre which would accept as one of its supporting attractions a tall, skinny beanpole of a youth who, sporting a bowler hat and umbrella, began his act with the words, 'I expect you're wondering why I sent for you.'

Anything To Get Into Show Business

My first professional engagement was with a gent by the name of Carroll Levis who ran what I suppose was the first of the nationwide amateur talent contests which hit Britain back in the 1930s.

When I joined him in 1951 his radio programmes were a pop success, and his touring shows packed the music halls. His slogan was: 'The discoveries of today are truly the stars of tomorrow.' But not that many of them ever did become stars. Offhand I can think of only one Carroll Levis discovery who had become by definition a star — Jim Dale. Levis unearthed a lot of talent, it's true, but there's a mysterious chemistry at work where stardom is concerned and it hasn't much to do with 'local boy makes good'.

I worked for him for a time as road manager, holding auditions in every town we visited, staging mini talent contests and passing the more promising discoveries up the line to Carroll for national exposure on radio, or at least a spot on his big shows at the number one variety theatres. I don't know what the rest of the world was singing in 1952, but at those auditions everyone sang either 'Bless This House' or 'Oh My Beloved Father'. Auditioning, on average, a hundred hopefuls a week you develop a callousness towards aspiring talent that verges on the brutal. Many poor singers never got further than 'Bless this . . .' or 'Oh my beloved . . .' before I gave them the traditional 'thank you — we'll let you know'. On bad days the poor wretches wouldn't get further than 'Bless . . .' or 'Oh . . .' before their hopes were dashed by the heartless villain in the stalls.

But the joy that sprang in my heart when someone produced a novelty item or a new idea was enormous. I've sat watching an aspiring acrobat clambering on and falling off a unicycle for twenty minutes on end — with a sensation of pure pleasure. A dog act where the dog was overcome by stage fright and just stood on the stage shivering, was nectar; and one red-letter day a contortionist (to the strains of 'A Pretty Girl Is Like A Melody') became locked in an extremely bizarre position and had to be carried to the local cottage hospital to be unravelled. These made up for the hours of 'Oh My Beloved Father', but were all too rare.

The high-water mark from the point of view of the student of the esoteric was when a comedian in Darlington, at the end of each joke, pressed a button concealed in his trouser pocket and his eye lit up. Truly. He had a glass eye into which he'd put a small light bulb, wired it up to a pocket battery and — hey presto! The sheer horror of his grisly partially-illuminated skull still gives me the shudders when I think of it.

I suppose it could be argued that he'd made a practical and sensible adaptation, and harnessed his disability for his own benefit and others' pleasure but you need to have an advanced taste for *kitsch* before the illuminated eye socket can be truly said to give deep enjoyment.

Why go to these lengths to get into show business? I suppose it's the desire not only to be different but to be seen to be special. Is it yet another aspect of the ascent of man? Some people do the football pools or study the F. T. Index. Others pull themselves together and go out and become fire-eaters or clog-dancers.

Take Kardomah — a variety artist of great skill and spectacular originality. His bill matter was Kardomah 'fills the stage with flags', — and that was exactly and precisely what he did. His costume was a maze of hidden pockets in which were concealed flags of all nations — every batten in the flies had more flags attached to them, and in a ground-cloth, a sort of carpet covering the stage, there were more hidden pockets also packed with flags. Kardomah, to the appropriate music, then produced flags. Hundreds and thousands of them, until quite literally the stage was full of flags. Curtain!

In twice-nightly variety having done it once, Kardomah would

16

have to do it again, and it took him the entire two hours between one appearance and the next to collect, refold and secrete these multifarious flags. Day in, day out, year in, year out. He made Sisyphus look like a dilettante.

Then there was a one-legged tightrope walker, whose name I forget, who turned his disability to advantage by dressing as a pirate; you could hear the crash when he fell off the wire — as he frequently did — all over the theatre. He was a New Zealander and as cheerful a man as I'd ever met, and, as his good humour was only equalled by his lack of balance, he needed to be cheerful.

My favourite one-legged entertainer was a negro tap-dancer who rejoiced in the name of Peg Leg Bates. A tap was fitted to the bottom of his peg and he would hammer out dance routines that were the envy of his fellow dancers. His biggest hazard was knot-holes in the stage. If he wasn't careful he'd disappear up to the knee and the pit orchestra would have to vamp until he'd extricated himself.

These men were pros. I cherish the memory of a week spent at Llanelly with, among others, a spoon-basher. Playing the spoons is an engaging if limited entertainment, and he was scheduled for five minutes tapping his anatomy with a pair of dessert spoons while the orchestra rattled through the Savoy American Medley.

Unfortunately a combination of circumstances had greatly depleted the local talent who were to be the Koh-i-nor in the crown of our week's presentation and having to provide a two-hour show twice nightly with only four acts proved a bit of a headache. The spoonologist, however, came to my rescue and volunteered to lengthen his act. I asked how? He told me, and I agreed. I had no option really — but have you ever heard 'Oh My Beloved Father' played on the spoons?

When I next ran into him some years later, he'd become a road-sweeper and seemed fairly content. He explained that he'd given up show business as it was too chancy. 'But,' he confessed, 'I miss the glamour.'

Escape

It's always seemed to me that the traditional ideas of escape — opening a coffee bar in the Atlas mountains, becoming a hashish exporter in Kabul or running a bicycle repair shop in Haiti — lead to a greater slavery than the life from which you wish to escape. Imagine yourself a bicycle repair man in Haiti — wonderful weather, carefree lackadaisical natives, a beautiful life-style, voodoo instead of Communion, reggae instead of Radio 1, hibiscus round the door. You have money (naturally! Without money dreams have a habit of staying dreams) so therefore you have position, prestige, and, at first, novelty value.

How many Caribbean islanders can boast of having their cycles repaired by a former chartered accountant or a women's knitting magazine television critic? Business will thrive. The Achilles heel of all such fantasies is that you drag your gross valise of attitudes, behaviour, prejudices and habits with you. You run out of brake blocks — the new saddles aren't delivered on time, inner tubes are perished by the climate or stolen by jolly lackadaisical natives, there are inadequate medical services, the CIA, ex-Nazi war criminals living next door, and *The Times* always arrives a week late. Now, of course, you dream of your desk at the knitwear magazine and the ordinary decencies of Ongar. Ironical, isn't it?

My only experience of true escapism was when I was on the music halls. The routine was that you played a week at, say, Llanelly and then spent Sunday on the train to Newcastle. A week in Byker would be followed by another in Truro and that would be followed by Oldham, Norwich, Carlisle, Eastbourne, Glasgow, Bilston and Swansea.

After a few months I'd travelled on almost every mile of track on British Rail. It sounds like hell, so where does escape come in? Well, the essence of escape is *hope*, and as the train pulled out — whether from Wolverhampton or Tonypandy — I felt a great liberation of spirit. One appalling week was behind me, the next could only be better. Maybe in the new town at the different theatre they'd laugh — perhaps we'd play to capacity business — maybe Val Parnell would be in town, catch the act and book me for the London Palladium. It had happened to others; it was possible it could happen to you.

Most of the talk among the older music hall performers in those days was of escape. They dreamed of chicken farms, tobacconist's shops, pubs, their own seaside concert party. To me who was just passing through — even in my daydreams I never saw myself as a star — it seemed that they aimed too high and wide of the mark. I could never quite imagine the jugglers and acrobats, magicians and tap-dancers being anything else but what they were. Perhaps they made it — but my guess is that they're still juggling, doing the splits, balancing on egg timers and time stepping to 'California Here I Come' in front of an audience of, I hope, enthusiastic OAPs.

I was content with my own weekly 'Escape From Colditz' game, of getting out and on to the next town, my disguise as a comedian unpenetrated, hoping that the train would pull out before the rush of feet and the yapping Alsatians which I imagined were there ready to drag me back to face another week of the Attercliffe Palace or the Grand, Byker. They never did catch me — I've never been back. That's one consolation! My escape route is still open and as I pant across the fields with my small cardboard suitcase of talent I still have hope that over the next rise will be the frontier and Freedom.

Small Top

We're told that the circus is in decline. Speaking personally, I wouldn't mind if the circus *never* came to town, for the sight of a group of elephants or horses doing tricks is, to me, as sad a sight as you can find. The human performers are a different case, as at least they have the option; and circus folk on the occasions I've met them (usually when they strayed on to variety bills back in the 1950s) seem cheerful and dedicated people. It's possible that they missed the caravan and canvas atmosphere of the circus and found theatres inhibiting, but if they did it didn't show. Mind you, it certainly inhibited a performing bear I once had to follow; although perhaps inhibit isn't the word I'm looking for, since the smell in the theatre was reminiscent of the Augean stables, and the top of the bill eventually complained that it was affecting his vocal chords. Talking of the Augean stables, the twelve labours of Hercules have always seemed to be the perfect circus bill. They were, you will remember:

1. *To slay the Nemean lion.*
2. *To kill the Lernean hydra.*
3. *To catch and retain the Arcadian stag.*
4. *To destroy the Erymanthian boar.*
5. *To cleanse the stables of King Augeas.*

19

6. *To destroy the cannibal birds of the Lake Stymphalis.*
7. *To take captive the Cretan bull.*
8. *To catch the horses of the Thracian Diomedes.*
9. *To get possession of the girdle of Hippolyta, Queen of the Amazons.*
10. *To take captive the oxen of the monster, Geryon.*
11. *To get possession of the apples of the Hesperides.*
    and —
12. *To bring up from the infernal regions the three-headed dog, Cerberus.*

That little lot ought to go down well after the Queen's speech on Christmas Day.

The top of the bill would, of course, be Hercules' horse, Arion. Arion had the power of speech, and its feet on the right side were those of a man. Chipperfields would pay real money for that sort of attraction. It's not *every* circus that has a star that can sing, dance *and* pull a caravan.

Great Days

If you'd had the misfortune to read as many show-business biographies and autobiographies as I have you would probably, like me, have come down with a bad case of blocked perceptions. It's not that the good people writing or written about are actually rascals masquerading as angels — far from it. Even Fred Karno, who according to his biographer was a perverted, sadistic swine, comes across finally as a poor soul dying, broke and forgotten. What comes through these 'show biz' biographies is the relentless glamour of the laughtermakers, and the alleged magic of the places in which they made people laugh. 'Ah,' they cry nostalgically, 'those lost Empires.'

The truth of the matter is that the variety theatres, at least the bit the performers inhabited, were like Victorian factories; less houses of joy than houses of correction. The walls were covered with faded and peeling instructions telling you what *not* to do. For instance — 'In case of Fire do *not* shout fire. Say quietly to your immediate superior, "Mr Robinson is in".' A fairly obtuse way of mentioning a conflagration. Another notice that appeared in some dressing-rooms was 'Do not stand in the wash-basins'. Chorus girls who disobeyed this edict were described as having been 'terribly lacerated', which doubtless they were. The point is that it highlights the shortage of washing facilities that caused the girls to stand in the basins in the first place. 'No cooking in the dressing-rooms' was another notice that appeared in some theatres. Theatres generally of the middle rank, I should add, as the top halls didn't generally book the type of act who would cook in the room, and the smaller places usually smelt so awful that you wouldn't have noticed the preparation of a complete Tandoori meal. Anybody observing flames licking around the proscenium arch in those theatres and saying to the stage manager 'Mr Robinson is in' would have been greeted with the dour response, 'Well he's the only bugger that is. The only show that's ever taken money here was *Soldiers in Skirts*.'

Soldiers in Skirts was a post-war phenomenon and it and its many imitators were shows in which the entire company were female impersonators. The idea sprang, of course, from the wartime Army amateur concert parties where, as there were no females adjacent to the front line, the ladies' parts were played by men. I dread to think of a regiment made up of the cast of *Soldiers In Skirts* who would shriek and titter through the stage door looking rather more feminine than they actually did on stage. The Duke of Wellington's 'I don't know if they'll frighten the enemy but by God they frighten me' was never more apt than with these particular soldiers. My guess was that they'd never got further than the Army medical before being returned sharply to Civvy Street.

In the distant days when I was a music-hall comedian, no bill was ever complete without a ventriloquist whose small partners would range from suitably adapted pocket handkerchiefs to life-size, if not life-like, octogenarian dummies. Some were good. Ray Alan, who I met around that time, has with *his* small partner, Lord Charles, become the most entertaining act of its kind in the English-speaking (without moving your lips) world. Then there was Señor Wences with, among other things, a head in a box ('All right?' he would ask. 'All right,' the head would reply), and Robert Lamouret with Dudule, a duck who lost an eye in the course of proceedings and spent a hilariously macabre five minutes looking for it. A one-eyed duck or a disembodied head may arouse compassion in some people, but most of the touring ventriloquists I met in the fly-blown incipient Bingo Halls of my variety days were terrible.

The point about ventriloquizing is that certain letters of the alphabet are extremely difficult to say without moving your mouth. B, F, M, P, V and W are especially hard, W coming out as 'duggleyew' if you're not careful. But the worse the Vent the more he'd want to attempt what his own common sense must have told him was beyond his powers. Thus the poor devils would end the act with songs like 'Carolina In The Morning' with the danger of strangulation never far away in the bit that goes (in ventriloquist-ese) 'gutterflies all clutter uk, and kiss each little gutterkuk . . .'

I loved the late Sandy Powell's comedy vent act. It was a classic, especially the bit where he asked his dummy, Sonny Jim, where he came from and the dummy answered with mind-splitting difficulty, 'Wolverhampton.' Pausing for the spots before his eyes to clear, Sandy Powell would say to the audience in a throaty aside, 'It's my own fault. I could have said Leeds.'

But for every Sandy Powell, Arthur Askey, Max Miller or Vic Oliver there was enough dross to create a new Spilsbury Down and usually these Empires and Palaces and Hippodromes were echoing vaults where the pit orchestra, had it contained musicians of a sufficient sensitivity, would have heard their wrong notes bouncing back to them from the back wall of the empty circle. To be fair, pit bands were sometimes amazingly good; one at Hull, I seem to remember, being excellent and the band at Attercliffe Palace, Sheffield, in the 1950s was a nest of trad jazz men who although they couldn't read music that well, were terrific when busking the accompaniment to a juggling routine or playing Basin Street Blues during the intermission. Attercliffe Palace was the theatre where Monday-morning band call was interrupted for twenty minutes while the Council Rodent Operatives, a couple resembling Kojak and Sergeant Crocker, squirted rat poison through every aperture in the theatre. Eventually they disappeared into the dressing-room of the dancing act and were never seen again. The dancers were a pair of nubile sisters whose bill matter 'four feet in perfect rhythm' told less than the truth. They'd have had a rough time had the Trades Description Act been in force, but the ugly one was quite a good hoofer and the pretty one was — well, pretty — so they worked with a fair degree of regularity.

Band calls were a great time for odd happenings; often half the band were missing, the bandsmen being only semi-pros and having to do a day in pit or factory before slipping a dinner jacket over their working trousers and making the evening hideous with their attempts to sight-read the score. In London the brass section were frequently members of one of the Guards bands stationed at Wellington Barracks and their speciality was to write messages on the band parts. You'd find scribbled notes like 'twelve minutes patter – bloody awful', or 'Cue goat in the blancmange chord in F segue I Want To Be Happy in two', or 'Six to four he's paid off by Wednesday' — or 'Who booked this load of rubbish?'

When I read books about the great stars and the great days of the music halls, I smile wryly. It's not for me to knock a boom industry, and if people hunger for something they believe once existed and is now gone, I'm not going to argue. There *were* great stars; I worked with many of them and once in a while — a long while — the magic *did* work. But for most of the time in most Music Halls in the majority of towns that I played it was hell, and when those of us who toured the halls meet and reminisce, we talk not of the good old days, but of the horror of it all. We laugh, of course, but it's the laughter of relief that the music hall is dead and gone.

Broadcasting

Most of what I think and believe about radio comedy is embodied in my book, *Laughter In The Air*. I grew up to the sound of those disembodied voices of the early broadcasters and even today I can recall the excitement of plays by L. Du Garde Peach, and the laughter generated by Claud Dampier, Gillie Potter, and Arthur Marshall. Arthur has since become a dear friend of both my wife and myself (they have a private and absurd postcard competition, each vying with the other for the most inappropriate card or the absurdest message — typically a picture postcard from Arthur of Marie Antoinette's enormous and elaborate bedroom at Versailles bearing the cheery note: 'Just a snap of one of my smaller guest rooms.') Then, in the 1930s, that is, my first stumbling attempts at humour were imitations of Arthur Marshall's guide mistresses, matrons and music teachers.

'Band Waggon' was best of all and to me Arthur Askey and Richard Murdoch were the funniest and freshest comedians of them all in the precarious days of 1938 and 1939. Of the wartime shows 'ITMA' was great, but I found 'Much Binding In The Marsh' better, and my subsequent years working for and enjoying the friendship of Kenneth Horne were the best years of my radio life.

It's surprising how much good radio and television survives the acid test of time and comes up gleaming, however old it is.

The coming of radio in the early 1920s was probably the most important event in mass communication since the invention of the printing press. In the aftermath of the Great War, at a time of national exhaustion and depression, radio was stimulating, lively and optimistic, and the BBC's motto 'Nation Shall Speak Peace Unto Nation' summed up the aspirations of the time, if not the realities.

The early broadcasters were enthusiastic and ingenious. They had to be. Resources were limited, techniques were primitive, and the nature of what was to be broadcast was pure guesswork. Everybody 'mucked in' — the tiny BBC staff, their friends and acquaintances. The ten-shilling licence fee quickly produced a sufficient income for rapid expansion, but attempts to lure the big names of variety and legitimate theatre to the infant medium were thwarted by the impressarios of the day. They felt, and I suppose that it was an understandable fear, that if their stars could be heard free no one would pay to see them in the theatre. Ironically the reverse turned out to be true and a radio 'name' meant big box office.

A more rational fear that many comedians shared was that material once heard on the wireless could never be used again, and that an act that had done service for years on tour could, after one broadcast, become obsolete.

Musicians and singers weren't inhibited in the same way and although there are a finite number of times that one can hear 'Drake's Drum', or Nevin's 'Narcissus' with enjoyment, music libraries tend to be vast while jokes were then (and are still today) in comparatively short supply. It wasn't until the 1940s that script writing became recognized as a profession at all, and not until Ted Kavanagh created his script agency did it become a *respectable* profession.

Ted Kavanagh was a gifted New Zealander who gave up his studies as a medical student to become a free-lance journalist in the 1920s, and in 1925 wrote a script on spec for a comedian whom he'd heard and who had impressed him: Tommy Handley. The script was a success and a partnership and friendship was created that in time produced one of the great classics of radio comedy, 'ITMA', and only ended with the death of Tommy Handley in 1949.

Most comedy in the twenties and thirties was mainly in the hands of soloists, men like Gillie Potter whose accounts of the happenings in the fictitious village of Hogsnorton and of the local squire, Lord Marshmallow, were immensely popular, and whose invariable opening line, 'Good Evening, England. This is Gillie Potter speaking to you in English,' soon made him a household name.

Then there were John Henry, Norman Long, Charles Penrose 'the laughing policeman', Sandy Powell, whose 'Can you hear me mother?' was one of the first of the best-remembered of radio catchphrases. The Western Brothers, Murray and Mooney, Will Fyffe, Robb Wilton, Suzette Tarri, Claud Dampier, and Billie Carlisle, Beryl Orde, Bebe Daniels and Ben Lyon, Vic Oliver, Tommy Trinder, Max Miller, Elsie and Doris Waters, and many others besides, made the successful leap from the theatre to the microphone and became established stars.

So, too, did Arthur Marshall with his deliciously funny female impersonations, Hermione Gingold both as herself and in a burlesque of a lady concert violinist with the bizarre name of Mrs Pullpleasure, Jeanne de Casalis as a dizzy housewife aptly named Mrs Feather, and the enigmatic storyteller, A. J. Alan (real name Leslie Harrison Lambert) were all attracting enormous audiences in the thirties, but the undoubted and resounding hit of pre-war radio was 'Band Waggon' starring Arthur Askey and Richard Murdoch. The irreverent and mischievous humour of Askey and Murdoch and the gallery of characters invented for the series, Mrs Bagwash and her daughter Nausea, Lewis the goat, Basil and Lucy the pigeons and the saga of life in their totally fictitious flat in Broadcasting House injected something brand new into British radio comedy.

The men behind the development of high-quality radio entertainment were themselves drawn from the theatre. They included Harry S. Pepper, Eric Maschwitz, John Watt, Pat Hillyard, Gordon Crier, Vernon Harris, and the man who perhaps more than any other helped to create modern radio and television comedy, Ronnie Waldman. He summed up the great success of 'Band Waggon' when he said: 'Its great quality was that it created something you felt you could see; characters that you could picture even if they were invisible, or indeed non-existent.' In fact, that sums up all the great radio comedies. The small girl who, when asked why she preferred radio to television, said 'because the scenery is nicer' was saying no more than the truth. Listeners create for themselves an environment which can't help but be ideal. The imagination can transcend any studio setting.

During the war, radio ruled supreme and the pinnacle of success was reached by the incredible 'ITMA' which, with its gallery of characters, its dozens of catchphrases, its cheery iconoclastic *bonhomie* and, above all, Tommy Handley, became a national institution. Handley was never a great success in any other field of entertainment, but on radio he was king. For the ten years that 'ITMA' ran it was loved by all (or nearly all — Professor Joad, a pundit of the day, claimed that he'd never heard the programme) and established standards that have rarely been equalled and seldom surpassed since. The three men mainly responsible, Francis Worsley, the producer, Ted Kavanagh, the writer, and Handley, the star, were an unbeatable combination.

With the coming of peace in 1945 two things happened — both incidentally caused by the war. One was the arrival of a whole new group of performers, writers and producers — men who had developed their skills in troop concerts and barrack-room entertainments and who breathed new life into show business. The second was the vastly improved technology. Sound recording, thanks to tape, became more sensitive and flexible, and when television staggered blinking into the light after its enforced wartime shutdown, the only thing to delay its eventual dominance over all the other entertainment media was shortage of cash and public indifference.

In the early 1950s with those two items out of the way, television blossomed. The coming of commercial television in 1955 speeded the process, competition sharpening the protagonists' wits, and with the arrival of colour the pattern that we see today became firmly established. Not that with the coming of television radio had crawled away quietly to die. The fifties were a golden age for radio comedy. 'Take It From Here', 'The Goon Show', 'In All Directions', 'Breakfast With Braden', 'Life Of Bliss', 'Ray's A Laugh', and 'Educating Archie' were all successful. 'Variety Bandbox' gave the world the sprawlng talents of Frankie Howerd. Domestic comedy thrived with 'Life With The Lyons', 'Meet The Huggetts,' and 'The Clitheroe Kid'. Ronnie Taylor's 'Variety Fanfare' put a new kick into an old formula. Even 'Workers' Playtime' was still going strong and continued, in fact, until the mid-sixties. Best of all, perhaps, was 'Hancock's Half Hour'. A list of the stars and writers who made these shows and who were made by them reads like a roll of honour. Frank Muir and Denis Norden, Spike Milligan, Harry

Secombe, Peter Sellers, Peter Jones and Peter Ustinov, Max Bygraves, Dick Emery, George Cole, Eric Sykes, Sid Colin, Hattie Jacques, Tony Hancock, Kenneth Williams, Ray Galton and Alan Simpson, June Whitfield, Jimmy Edwards, and the rest, learned their stuff standing at the microphone at the Paris, the Playhouse, Aeolian One, and the other converted cinemas, theatres and concert halls where with the dedicated and skillful producers, studio managers, grams operators, and sound effects men, they turned those pages of typescript into the stuff that dreams are made of.

Many of the radio top-liners made the switch to television with no apparent effort, and most are happily and prosperously working there today but comedy stars made entirely by television are surprisingly few in number. Morecambe and Wise have done radio, but they would be the first to admit that it was television that made them the stars they are today. BBC, ATV, then BBC again and now Thames have each sampled the charisma and pulling power of Eric and Ernie — men who can generate more laughter than any two human beings have any right to. Benny Hill is television's own son, astoundingly successful and seemingly evergreen (even if perhaps the green is tinged with blue). Ronnie Barker and Ronnie Corbett, whether solo or together, are consummate performers, with Barker perhaps having the edge, thanks to his devastatingly accurate character studies in such delights as 'Open All Hours', 'Porridge', and 'Going Straight'.

Mike Yarwood, John Inman, Johnny Speight, Warren Mitchell, and Penelope Keith, while successful in other fields, too owe much of their success to television and, of course, Monty Python's Flying Circus could only have existed on the screen.

There's no doubt that the Python phenomenon is one of the most significant things to have happened to television in recent years. Other shows have been as popular, indeed in terms of audience measurement many are *more* popular. But while most comedy confirms one prejudice or another, the Pythons offer a sort of moral do-it-yourself kit where the viewer is invited to make his own decisions. Their popularity both on television and in the cinema proves the Python team have won the hearts and minds of their audience, and while other comedians and impresarios, their heads hardened in Moss Empires and provincial clubs, may shrug them off as a passing fad, no programme maker should ignore what made Python work. They are a group of free-thinking, intelligent and self-critical men — but they're not alone in that. The important thing is that they run their own on-screen affairs and in their early days, many years ago now, they were never censored nor even guided. They were told how much money was available and what facilities they could use — given an excellent producer and allowed to let rip. Once they were on the screen the BBC kept faith with the team, and in spite of the occasional hiccup backed them up to the moment they became a popular success. After that everybody saw the point.

The question is often asked why the BBC is so much more successful at comedy than ITV. Well if it is, and it's a debatable point, then it's because of the freedom I've just described. The BBC has no rigid show business orthodoxy, no preconceptions of what will work and what will not. It makes shows, by and large, on the premise that it 'seems a good idea', knowing that the good idea will succeed or fail quite arbitrarily. It always has and it always will; nobody can guarantee in advance the success of an untried comedy idea. Anybody who thinks he can is a fool; anyone who tries deserves our respect. You've got to be a brave man to work in comedy — or terminally insane.

Going Commercial

I started working for Independent Television before it opened — for free, I might add. They used to hold auditions in a suite of studios off Kensington High Street, and there one would go to audition for the new, exciting commercial telly. I realize now that those auditions were, in fact, used to train directors, floor managers and vision mixers and whilst, no doubt, talented newcomers *were* spotted and subsequently seen on the screen, I was not among them.

I was a stand-up comedian in those days, working mainly in music halls, doing the occasional radio variety show, and just beginning to write. I wrote because I couldn't afford script writers, but I was lucky with my friends, John Law, Bill Craig, and Marty Feldman, who pushed and pulled my act around and bullied me into — well, adequacy, I think, would be fair. Also word of my existence eventually reached Val Parnell, at that time boss of ATV, and in 1956 I was given the summer replacement spot for ATV's 'Jack Jackson Show'.

Jackson was one of the hits of TV at that time and his show, featuring Paddy O'Neil and Glen Mason, was the big event of Sunday nights, a zany mix of comedy and music which was made in a tiny studio in Foley Street behind the Middlesex Hospital, and was, in its day, the funniest programme on the air. It was fast, original and iconoclastic, virtues as rare then as they are now on British television. Anyway, I was to replace Jackson which was rather like expecting a rowing-boat to replace the *QE2*, and one critic observed in a masterpiece of understatement that the material was 'a bit puerile'.

By and large, comedy on ITV in its early years was streets ahead of the BBC who hadn't had time to regroup and fight back. Top shows included ATV's 'Joan and Leslie', starring Joan and Leslie Randall and written by Law and Craig, Granada's 'Army Game' with Michael Medwin, William Hartnell (subsequently the first Dr Who), Geoffrey Sumner, Bernard Bresslaw, and Alfie Bass, written by Sid Colin, Lew Schwarz, Maurice Wiltshire and Larry Stephens — and Rediffusion's 'Dickie Henderson Show'. These programmes, along with variety shows and quizzes, helped ITV to a massive seventy per cent of the viewing audience. 'Sunday Night At The London Palladium' (with first Tommy Trinder then Bruce Forsyth, and later Norman Vaughan, compèring and running the Beat The Clock spot) was the most broadly popular of the big variety shows, but Granada's 'Chelsea At 9', and the many Jack Hylton packages shown by Rediffusion were as good in their way, and ATV's 'Saturday Spectacular', written by and featuring Eric Sykes, was possibly the best of the lot. It was in this series, surely, that the classic Eric Sykes preposterous send-up of an army marching display first saw the light of day. That routine — Sykes, Harry Secombe and Norman Vaughan solemnly marching and countermarching — would go into any compilation of the best moments of ITV.

Meanwhile, back at the Took — I was really in the soup after the abortive 'Round About Ten' (as the Jack Jackson replacement show was called) and it wasn't until 1959 that a commercial company ventured to use my services again. Producer Peter Croft wanted some comedy on his late night chat and music show, 'Late Extra', and stuck for someone to amuse the throng he tried me. The spot worked and he asked me to act the part of a barman who would from time to time make topical quips and comment on the rest of the show. The two weeks I was originally booked for were

30

extended to six, then to thirteen and I finally appeared for forty-two consecutive weeks, most of them live, and left only when the strain of being both topical and live brought me out in a nervous rash.

By then, Marty Feldman and I were writing for Granada's 'Army Game' series and in particular for the leading performers in the series, Alfie Bass and Bill Fraser. By the spring of 1960, Granada wanted to give Bass and Fraser their own series and to continue 'The Army Game' with Dick Emery in the lead. The new show was called, at one time, 'Alf and Bill', then 'Nice And Ugly', but mercifully arrived on the screen as 'Bootsie and Snudge'.

In those days, ITV comedy shows ran on the American pattern — thirty-nine episodes at a time being quite common. We certainly did thirty-nine programmes in the first series of Bootsie, with Marty and me contributing twenty-five of them, the others being written by John Antrobus, Ray Rigby, Bill Craig, David Cumming and Derek Collyer.

In the 1961–62 season, the series was only twenty-four programmes long — a blessed relief, except that we had to soldier through a long Equity strike (Equity quite properly wanted a bigger stake in what Lord Thompson of Fleet had called a licence to print money) using only the four actors under contract — Bass, Fraser, Robert Dorning and Clive Dunn. We used every permutation of being locked in, locked out and being stranded in the middle of nowhere — soliloquies abounded and, good as the actors were, it was agony to work under such restrictions. When finally the strike was settled, Marty and I celebrated by writing a story with eighteen speaking parts, a parody of Alfred Hitchcock's *Rear Window*.

There were one hundred episodes of 'Bootsie and Snudge' altogether, and I was associated with them all in one way or another. I can't remember what was happening in the rest of ITV during that period, and, in fact, I'd be hard put to it to remember what happened anywhere else on earth, so involved was I with the day-to-day affairs of Bootsie and Snudge. When Granada closed their Chelsea studio and shifted all their production to Manchester, Marty and I moved over to the BBC, then back to ATV to work for a season on 'The Braden Beat' — as 'The Esther Rantzen Show' was called in those days. We were told later that the production team had had a bet on which one of us was Took and which was Feldman. Such is the anonymity of the script writer.

My next gainful employment in commercial television was with Rediffusion at the end of that company's contract. I then moved to

ABC, for which company I script edited a Tommy Cooper series and a series called 'Horne A'Plenty', starring the late Kenneth Horne. When Rediffusion and ABC merged to become Thames Television I worked for Philip Jones (their Controller of Light Entertainment) as comedy consultant, then went back to the BBC, went to Hollywood briefly to work on 'Rowan and Martin's Laugh In', returned to England and the vacant chair of Head of Light Entertainment at London Weekend Television, resigned after a year when they sacked my boss, Stella Richman (it seemed to be a tradition!*) and have since worked mainly for the BBC.

My most recent experience of ITV was a series made in May and June 1975 for Yorkshire Television and called 'N.U.T.S.' It was shown in October and November and I didn't know when I wrote the first version of this whether it was going to be rosebuds or rhubarb. Time and the viewers would tell.**

It seems to me that today there's very little difference between comedy on BBC or IBA, particularly as writers and performers frequently commute between the two, but in the early years of commercial television there's no doubt that men with the drive and insight of Val Parnell, Bill Ward, Peter Eton and the rest changed and improved our expectations of what comedy on television could be like.

*Frank Muir was the first H.O.L.E. He resigned when Michael Peacock was sacked. I was succeeded by Michael Grade, who was in turn replaced by David Bell.
**YTV liked the series — not much, but they liked it enough to have a second bash with a new title (Took & Co.), a new cast, and a new producer. The successor failed miserably.

Love That Soap

It's strange but true that while commercial television in Great Britain has consistently produced successful soap operas, such as 'Coronation Street', 'Crossroads', and 'Emmerdale Farm', 'Emergency – Ward 10', 'Crown Court', and 'Bouquet Of Barbed Wire', the BBC never really got its act together in this area. It tried hard enough with epics like 'United', the story of a Midlands soccer club, and 'Compact', a long-running saga of life in the world of magazine publishing, and more recently the much-mocked 'Triangle', the saga of life on a car ferry ploughing around the North

Sea apparently bereft of crew, passengers or owners, except a tiny handful of people engaged in steamy romance, petty theft, or boardroom double dealing. Where the BBC has succeeded is in cornering the market in American soaps. 'Dallas' and 'Dynasty' are perhaps the most famous, but there was 'Knot's Landing' too, and other minor epics that still attract big audiences. In the early 1980s there was an attempt to find the British equivalent and one of the manifestations of this attempt was a serial written by the author of the extremely successful 'Bouquet Of Barbed Wire', Andrea Newman. It was called 'Mackenzie'.

I must confess that 'Mackenzie' came as a shock.

No, I wasn't outraged by its semi-explicit love scenes, or the seemingly endless combinations and permutations of the couplings of the characters, the lovelessness or the violence or the betrayals that made up most of the plot. The shock was to see how well it was made, and the care and attention and money that'd gone into its making. Why, it was *good*! Well, not *that* good. Its pace and predictability were that of a well-maintained grandfather clock, but the swing of the pendulum from one sequence to another, and the sonorous ticking of the plot, were undeniably hypnotic. What's more, it was a very moral tract. Apart from the occasional moment of what in a world other than 'Mackenzie' would be called 'a bit of the other', there's not a lot that couldn't be written in poker-work and hung in a nursery. The goodies were clearly going to succeed, the baddies just as clearly going to get their come-uppance. This sense of morality was made doubly effective by the fact that it was all happening to a Scottish family, the Mackenzies. They were a family that, had they not been invented by the skilful Andrea Newman, would be more concerned with healthy walks, salmon fishing, porridge oats, and watching Andy Stewart on television. As it was, they spent their time being emotionally pulled through a hedge backwards. There seemed no scene without its crisis, and watching you got the uneasy feeling that the very passersby might get dragged into it. I feared for the postman every time he knocked at the door, half expecting one or other of the ladies in the show to appear in a flimsy negligée, beckon him in and offer to set him up in his own post office.

Not that anything as frivolous as that was likely to happen. 'Mackenzie' was, as far as I saw, entirely without any trace of humour. Just as well, probably. Once you introduce humour into such situations there's no knowing where it will end. The whole thing could have ground to a halt in paroxysms of helpless laughter as cast, writer, producer and audience fell about at the silliness of it all.

I'm not complaining. After all, there's so much to laugh at in the world these days that an occasional moment of solemnity does you good. The trouble is that one ill-considered line in an otherwise serious piece can ruin it for ever. I remember vividly in 'Coronation Street', some years ago, a distrait young man delivering himself of the epic line 'If I can't have Elsie Tanner, nobody shall,' a phrase that left me not only speechless but helpless with laughter, and since then I've never been able to take soap operas seriously — if at all.

There was a moment in an episode of 'Mackenzie' that edged perilously close to Morecambe and Wise when in a restaurant (the food, like the emotions of the characters, flambéed) Mackenzie's ex-wife, Jean, told her schoolmaster lover that she wasn't going to marry him after all. In the pause for the shock-horror reaction as the poor chap absorbed this bombshell, the head waiter approached with the line, 'Is everything all right, sir?' Well, I know dramatic irony when I see it, but it was a close-run thing.

But let us not beat about the bush. This was no Grove Family that we were watching. There was not a soul in sight who wasn't lacerated with guilt, lust, anger or fear. Strokes and heart attacks abounded, watched pots were for ever boiling over, and destiny hovered among the doom-laden cello music of the sound track waiting to strike down the fondest hope. Like everyone else, I was dying to find out what happened next. Perhaps Mackenzie would go into business with JR. My word, that'd set the pulses racing.

But after 'Mackenzie', what? Love among the speculative builders and property tycoons of the 1960s is, I would have thought, a fairly limited vein to exploit. Would it be royalty next — no, we've had that already, with 'Edward and Mrs Simpson'. The loves of the Popes? A tv series about the Borgias was nearing completion and was about to spring the seamy doings of renaissance Italy upon us. The future where anything can happen and probably won't is covered by 'Blake's Seven'. Love among the bedpans is amply described in 'Angels'.

As in so many other areas of our national life, the lead should be given by the government. The pungent compost of cabinet meetings during Labour's time in office is already yielding a rich

34

harvest of soap situations via the diaries of those present at the time, and I'm sure the present administration can do just as well. Let's hop into Dr Who's police box and time-travel, let's say ten years into the future, and peer back. What will we find?

The events of the early 1980s as seen through the eyes of Andrea Newman, could not fail to be a winner. Let me suggest a storyline. A shy, young monetarist arrives in London to take up residence in her new home. Her bluff, no-nonsense hubby feels a bit out of it as our heroine is caught up in the intoxicating whirl of the society round: here photographed kissing a pig, there talking to a trade unionist about his fecklessness. Captivated at first by the gay, young Minister for the Arts with the world's definitive collection of Queen Victoria's underwear, she jets around the world deferred to by peers of the realm, hobnobbing with presidents, and telling the French where to get off. Other characters could be a son, who is a fashion model, a daughter who isn't, a crusty old retainer or two, a grim-visaged former boss waiting in the wings in the hope of seeing her discredited. Be they old queens or young ruffians, our heroine mingles with the highest in the land, and yet deep down she's just a simple, good natured lass from the provinces who believes in two things — freedom and Friedman.

Believe me, it's a winner. I can imagine the publicity handout: 'See giant businesses topple, see our heroine's political rivals in disarray, see the wets, the moles, and the work-shy routed.' I'm telling you — it's bigger than *Gone With The Wind*.

The Identikit Soap Opera

I have, in fact, written what I consider the blueprint for the perfect British soap opera.

> *MEMO*
> To: The Managing Director. Rockall Television.
> From: United Computer Script Writing Company Limited.
> Subject: Proposed new twice-weekly tv serial.

Starting from your brief which indicated you wished to introduce a new serial of the type colloquially known as 'soap opera', we at United Computer Scripts have examined the existing products on the market, and have noted certain facts about current series of this type: 'Crossroads', 'Emmerdale Farm', and 'Coronation Street'. Our findings suggest that the cast should number 15.3 people. Of the sample tested week ending 5 February, 'Crossroads' had 20 people, 'Coronation Street' 17 people, and 'Emmerdale Farm' 8, thus the average is 15.3 and should contain as many variations of age and social class as possible.

The surnames should be of two syllables, eg. Sugden, Odgen, Hunter, Parker, Potter, Bradshaw — Christian names too tend to be of two syllables, eg Annie, Elsie and Betty, but monosyllables seem to be preferred (eg Jim, Meg, Stan, Jill, etc.). We have also noted that the more successful series have a provincial background. We assume this to be because social changes in these areas are less rapid than in the capital, and in addition a provincial locale provides the possibility of aspiration, eg 'I'm chucking this and going to live in London.' (There is no recorded case of a participant in a series set in London saying 'I'm chucking this and going to live in Eccles.')

In search of the ideal soap opera, we at UCSW then began to consider possible locations in which to set our series. We discarded a lighthouse as being insufficiently flexible for long-running dramatic action. The light is either on or it's off and that's it. While it is possible for the 15-plus cast envisaged to be present in the lighthouse, they could only be there as survivors of a shipwreck, illegal immigrants, or squatters, none of which possibilities was felt to get the audience identification which is the core of a successful soap opera.

In considering other locations, we discarded a home for distressed gentlefolk, a prison, a labour exchange, and a battery chicken farm because of their lack of immediate identification for a mass audience. Some branch of the Armed Forces was considered, but it was felt to be adequately covered, some might say more than adequately, in other series (eg 'Sailor', 'Warship', 'Dad's Army', 'Get Some In') as indeed are the activities of the police who appear, on superficial examination, to be under contract to the BBC.

After much discussion, the UCSW team came up with the following suggestions which I append for your approval.

Title: T'Corner Shop
The story concerns the day to day adventures of the owners and customers of a typical corner grocery shop situated on the outskirts of a small farming community near Walsall.

The Principal Characters

Maggie Oakroyd Mid-fifties, the owner of the shop. On the surface a termagant, but underneath she has a heart of gold, always ready to help pensioners and the unemployed. In spite of that she has no time for social security scroungers. She likes young people 'so long as they've got clean hair' but has no time for football hooligans or socialists who, she thinks, should be locked up. She is married to —

Jeb Oakroyd Maggie's second husband. (Her first met a tragic end when he fell into a grain silo on their honeymoon in 1947.) Jeb is a simple, no-nonsense, please-yourself, call-a-spade-a-spade chap, happier in his pigeon loft than in t'shop. Believes all blackies should be sent home except the local cricket team's opening bat and leg spin bowler, who is —

Amin Patel Softly spoken and mild mannered (except on cricket field) an ex-Ugandan Asian who works in a nearby dye works as well as driving the shop's delivery van. He's saving up to open a Tandoori takeaway in the village. Goes to night school to improve his English, but still uses amusing antique anglicisms, such as 'well bowled, old sport', 'wizard prang', 'can I do you now, sir', and 'how's your belly off for spots'. He is emotionally attached to —

Fanny Beaver The village good-time girl. An intensely beautiful, wayward and magnetic titian-haired creature of 55 who has kept her wonderful figure, thanks to a foundation garment apparently made by the British Steel Corporation. (NB This may seem incongruous, but our researches reveal that most soap operas have this type of sex goddess in their cast.)

Early in the series, we meet:
Jim Beaver Fanny's illegitimate son (his father was a US

serviceman stationed in the area) on leave from the Royal Navy and thinking of joining the local constabulary when his service is completed and thus replacing:

Old Fred   The village policeman. Dull but reliable.

Then there's:

Old Bert   A wise old farmhand. Reliable but dull.

Old Sid   A stupid old farmhand. The butt of —

Old Ted   Landlord of the Goat And Trouserpress, the local pub. His speciality is keeping real ale for passing journalists and drinking bottled Double Diamond himself. Often to be seen in the snug of the Goat And Trouserpress is:

Lady Vicuna Stavely, JP   The Lady of the Manor, who finds a strange affinity with Maggie Oakroyd, though they are from different ends of the social scale. Lady Vicuna spends most of her time worrying about the madcap antics of:

The Hon. Peter Staveley   Her ne'er do well son. (Hobbies: hang gliding, stock car racing, and flower arrangement.) Whenever the Hon. Peter gets in a scrape (eg found intoxicated in a transvestite club in Newton-le-Willows) he is invariably saved from public disgrace by:

Ramsbottom   The Staveley's unflappable chauffeur, whose suave exterior hides the fact that he's an ex-convict and the real father of:

Nyrere Thicket   A young village girl whose ambition is to emigrate to Australia and make a new life for herself. Her secret shame is known only to:

Sylvia Anthrax   The district nurse, who knows everyone's private affairs but keeps them to herself until she can contain herself no longer and unburdens herself to:

James Ferret   A vet who is secretly a best-selling novelist writing under the pseudonym of Stanley McMurtry, and using the village folk as his models.

That completes the list of the requisite 15 characters; the ·3 is taken care of by the fact that Nyrere Thicket is three months pregnant. By whom, we shall discover as the series progresses.

The stories for 'T'Shop' should be in line with the other main contenders in the field and be simple, uncomplicated and easily extendable. We fed all our information into the computer and append the following print-out:

'During a village cricket match, a loose ball bowled by Amin Patel is struck for six by the Hon. Peter Staveley who has turned out for the Visitors as they've arrived a man short. The ball crashes through the window of the snug at the Goat And Trouserpress spattering Old Bert, Old Sid, Old Ted, Fanny Beaver, and Lady Vicuna with broken glass. Some moments later, Fanny complains of severe abdominal pains. Has she ingested broken glass in the meat pie she was eating at the time of the cricket-ball incident?

'Nurse Anthrax is on a case at an outlying farm, so James Ferret, the vet (who's been fielding at long leg) is summoned. Unused to human ailments, he is nonplussed, but the indefatigable Maggie Oakroyd suggests an X–ray. They carry the comatose figure of Fanny to the Staveley Rolls Royce, and the suave Ramsbottom whisks the party to Ferret's surgery.

'On arrival they surprise Nyrere and Jim Beaver in a hot embrace behind the sterilizer. They explain that they were sheltering from a sudden summer storm and had removed their clothes to dry them. It's clear from James Ferret's reaction that beneath his calm exterior, the vet is a seething mass of twisted desire — but for which of the lovers? Meanwhile, the seething mass of Fanny Beaver is X–rayed and found to have swallowed not broken glass but a two-inch hoop ear-ring of the type only sold in t'corner shop. Clearly, there was a foreign body in the meat pie. Is Maggie Oakroyd guilty of negligence under the Shops and Catering (Processed Meat Amendment) Act of 1912? Was it an act of sabotage designed to discredit Maggie and close t'shop?

James Ferret remembers Amin Patel and the Hon. Peter Staveley in deep and furtive conversation before the match. Was Amin's long hop and the Hon. Peter's mighty six pure chance? What were Nyrere and Jim really doing in Ferret's surgery? Before the various cross-currents of doubt and suspicion are resolved, it's learned that Jeb Oakroyd has inadvertently fallen down a flooded mineshaft. Can he be rescued before the gritty waters engulf him? Maggie enlists the help of the local WI who form a human chain and . . .'

We regret to inform you that at this point the computer exploded. Pending the arrival of new parts, we beg to conclude our submission.

Donald G. Panderbody
for United Computer Scripts Limited

History Of The World So Far

The BBC have had such success with drama series in which large slices of history have been reduced to an evening's viewing that there are bound to be more of the same in the years to come.

Bold though these ventures are, the question is: 'Are they bold enough?' Greater efficiency and increased output are what's required in this country today, and with that in mind I offer a blueprint for more history in less time. So here goes with — 'The World So Far'.

Scene 1   *Fade up:* The Dawn of Creation. Day Seven. God (*Timothy West*) having created all the fishes and water for them to swim in, decides to take a day off and go fishing. Realizing He has nobody to tell about the one that got away, creates Adam (*Michael Parkinson*).

Scene 2   Adam and Eve (*Barbara Cartland*) in the Garden of Eden. The serpent gives Eve the apple — she eats it and starts sinning all over the garden (with Adam, of course). God, seeing that it's a bit pointless to have sin if no one knows about it, creates Nigel Dempster.

Scene 3   Monty Python's Old Testament with John Cleese as Lot, Graham Chapman as Lot's wife, Terry Jones as Onan, and special guest appearance of David

40

Frost as the Seven Plagues of Egypt.

Scene 4   Julius Caesar (*John Inman*) invades Britain in search of M & S knitwear. Returns to Rome with chunky sweater and cashmere cardigan which are mothproof, shrinkproof but, alas, not daggerproof — dies.

Scene 5   England invaded by Scots, Picts, Jutes, Angles, Saxons, Danes, and Vikings. Boadicea (*Penelope Keith*) calls for stricter immigration laws.

Scene 6   1066. Tostig of Northumbria (*Brian Clough*) defeated by Harold (*Lawrie McMenemy*) at Stamford Bridge. Harold reported as saying, 'I am over the moon.' Tostig: 'I'm as sick as a parrot.'

Scene 7   The Dark Ages. So called on account of unofficial strike by some members of the ABS.

Scene 8   1508. Michaelangelo (*Humphrey Burton*) starts to paint ceiling of Sistine Chapel — not completed until 1512. Michaelangelo blames delay on late delivery of paint, work to rule of ladder holders, and snow on the points at Verona.

Scene 9   Henry VIII (*Les Dawson*) ascends throne with difficulty, owing to weight. Marries Katherine of Aragon, Anne Boleyn, Jane Seymour, Anne of Cleves, Katherine Howerd, Catherine Parr. Dies 1547. Doctors (*Little and Large*) diagnose surfeit of mothers-in-law.

Scene 10   The Elizabethan Age. Queen Elizabeth One (*Lorraine Chase*) greets return of Drake (*Charlie Drake*) from round-the-world trip with immortal words, 'Hello, sailor.' She rewards him for beating the Armada with a gift of gold codpiece and six penn'orth of chips.

Scene 11   Shakespeare (*Larry Grayson*) meets Anne Hathaway (*Isla St Clair*) at Mermaid Tavern; is inspired to write *As You Like It*. Her comments on his virility inspire a second play, *Much Ado About Nothing*, but nine months later a son is born, which inspires a play *All's Well That Ends Well*. Son later ascribed to Bacon (*Max Bygraves*).

Scene 12 The Commonwealth under Cromwell (*Frankie Howerd*) turns out to be all common and no wealth and, as a result, in 1660 Charles II (*Arthur Negus*) is restored to the throne.

Scene 13 1666. Great Fire of London. Started in Pudding Lane by one Obadiah Larkshaunch (*Kenneth Williams*), who is subsequently known as the Great Plague of London.

Scene 14 The American War of Independence won by the Americans and thus paves the way for Jumbo-burgers, Coca-Cola, the Ku-Klux-Klan, Richard M. Nixon, napalm, Bruce Forsyth on Broadway, the Mormon Tabernacle Choir, chewing-gum, and Bette Midler.

Scene 15 The French Revolution gives the world the phrase 'The French are revolting' which can be heard today whenever the subject of British lamb exports is raised.

Scene 16 The rise of Bonaparte (*Mike Yarwood*) otherwise known as the Little Corporal, The First Consul, Emperor Napoleon the First, and General de Gaulle. Famous for putting his hand under his coat and saying 'Not tonight, Josephine' (*Shirley Bassey*). Beaten on the playing fields of Eton by the Duke of Wellington (*Ronnie Corbett*) who gives his name to the Wellington boot, and over two thousand public houses.

Scene 17 Victoria and Albert (*Pearl Carr and Teddy Johnson*) start the fashion for happily married royalty, which persists to the present day. Have many children, grandchildren, etc., most of whom will one day be featured in television series. Queen Victoria coins the phrase, 'We are not amused' (subsequently adopted as the slogan of the League of Television Critics) and in consequence, Peel reforms the Corn Laws.

Scene 18   The Twentieth Century. Featuring highlights of the past seventy-nine years, including in 1903 Wilbur and Orville Wright's first flight in heavier-than-air machine. In 1904, James Barrie writes Peter Pan. First flight of heavier-than-air fairy. Later flights of heavier-than-air fairies include Burgess and Maclean 1951, and Kim Philby 1963.

1921: The first Austin 7 seen on the roads.

1925: C.C. Magee invents the parking meter — thus giving the driver fourteen years to find somewhere to park.

1927: British Army abandons the lance.

1929: Ernest Hemingway writes *A Farewell To Arms*.

1935: Sir Malcolm Campbell breaks land-speed record at 301.7 mph. Leslie Hoare Belisha introduces 30 mph speed limit in built-up areas.

1936: John Maynard Keynes (*Stanley Unwin*) writes book in which he expounds his General Theory of Employment, Interest and Money.

1979: Sir Geoffrey Howe (*Harry Worth*) expounds *his* General Theory of Unemployment, 17 per cent Interest, and *No* Money.

There have been other events since then, but most of them are too horrible to contemplate — even on television.

People

There was a song popular in my youth that went 'Please don't talk about me when I'm gone', but it's only when a person is dead that you can see their achievements and their shortcomings in perspective, and can say things you couldn't have said to their face. All too often with the living we see only one aspect of the person. A man will seem totally different to his wife, his mistress, his children, his boss, his employees, and the professional at his golf club. And yet, of course, he is the same person, flawed maybe, but whole.

With show-business personalities these differences are even more pronounced, especially with funny men. It's almost impossible to imagine that the amiable chap who made you laugh so heartily in the cinema or theatre is a twisted neurotic in his private life. Many *are* however, and it's only by the perspective given by time that we can assess what their true contribution has been.

This section is about people I have known and liked. Some of it is based on film reviews, all of it is subjective and none of it pretends to be the definitive analysis of the person or their work.

44

Tony Hancock: Genius (Failed)

What makes a great comedian? Come to that, what makes any kind of comedian? It isn't the funny hat or the comical walk, it's the knack of being an interpreter of what we, the audience, believe but have never been able to put precisely into words.

The funny man talks of life and death, of hope and despair, of aspiration and failure, of thwarted hopes, of visions and desires. It's a rare gift: a mixture of insight, optimism, deep despair and self awareness that most of us don't possess, and it is ironic that these very qualities are the ones that often cause the comedian's final eclipse. It's as if he trips on the banana skin just once too often and kills himself. Not always literally, of course. Sometimes comics, for no obvious reason, just become unpopular. Perhaps they are superseded, as in the case of Derek Roy when Frankie Howerd first appeared on radio's 'Variety Bandbox' in 1948, bringing with him a different — and to the audience of those days a better — sort of humour: a humour more in touch with the lives, the hopes and fears of the listeners. It wasn't that Roy was worse — he just became obsolete. Howerd himself suffered a period of eclipse some years later and clawed his way back to popularity after a panicky period when it seemed that he had 'had it' as a major comic star.

Then again it's often the case that some indiscretion in the comic's private life becomes public property and people feel that their hero is somehow soiled, his *bonhomie* false, his jokes lies. Sometimes through age or neurosis comics just stop being funny, and sometimes comics are just not funny in the first place and have only been kept in the public eye by brilliant writers or producers. Occasionally comedians become so personally obnoxious that no one will employ them, and deprived of the oxygen of exposure their comic flair dies and they become forgotten.

The awful truth about comedians is that the public only want them to be funny. They don't want philosophers or pundits or politicians they just want a man to tell them something that will make them laugh.

In his all too short career Tony Hancock probably made more people laugh than any other British comedian, and the things he said then and the attitudes he struck remain in the mind as clearly as if they were coined yesterday. The news of his death, alone, in Australia in 1968 came as a terrible shock to many people. It wasn't just a comic who had died, it was a symbol.

Why did he die? What made him despair so much that he couldn't face living another day? Well, he was a sensitive man, that's obvious. He was a thoughtful man, and intelligent. He was also selfish, narcissistic, and desperately insecure. What is more, it is my belief (share it if you will) that he was ashamed of what he supposed was a weakness in himself — his lack of universality. He felt he ought to be able to do everything. Not only through vanity, but through a yearning to be renaissance man: artist, writer, philosopher, politician, and banker rolled into one. He wasn't content to be another Billy Russell, he wanted to be Bertrand Russell as well.

He felt that to *need* Sid James, Kenneth Williams, Alan Simpson and Ray Galton, Dennis Main Wilson, and Duncan Wood and the rest was a sign of a frightening inadequacy in himself. He genuinely wanted to go it alone. With all those excellent actors, writers and producers surrounding him he felt unable to achieve his full potential, and one by one he discarded them.

Intellectual snobbery played a part too. He chose Philip Oakes to write the film *The Punch And Judy Man* with him largely because Oakes was not only a journalist, critic and novelist but also a fine poet. Hancock felt the need to be near a man of such obviously distinguished intellectual and artistic qualifications, forgetting that Galton and Simpson had similar qualities, and forgetting incidentally, that anyone writing for Hancock would think, if only unconsciously, in the style and manner of the Galton and Simpson radio and television scripts.

As it happens, *The Punch And Judy Man* — while not a commercial success in the cinema — looks very good when it's shown on television. Tony Hancock needed the intimacy of radio and television, and though adequate on the big screen he was curiously diminished by its size. His art was the art of the close-up. His comedy could be compared to chamber music rather than to oratorio. His tragedy was that not content to be, as it were, Sir Thomas Beecham, he wanted to be Delius, Heifitz and Stradivarius too.

I can remember gossiping with Tony in a bar in Blindley Heath, near Lingfield in Surrey, where he lived for many years. We talked about working and personal relationships (my wife had been his secretary for a time), the problems of getting exactly what you wanted on to radio or the screen. We gossiped of this and that for an hour or so, and then he confessed his burning ambition. It was

46

to play King Lear with Richard Burton and Wilfrid Lawson, the three of them taking it turn and turn about to play Lear and Fool. One day Burton's Lear to Lawson's Fool, the next Lawson's Lear to Hancock's Fool, and so on. To this end Tony told me Herbert Morrison had promised to persuade the LCC, as it was then, to rebuild the Avenue Theatre in Shaftesbury Avenue. (It was at that time a bomb site used as a car park.) I expressed surprise and delight at the prospect. Privately I was profoundly dubious. Would such a venture see the light of day? *Could* such a project ever be realized? Reality said no, but the *idea* was magnificent. It was ideas in the end that strangled Tony Hancock. He didn't want to be just the selfish braggart of Railway Cuttings, the outsmarted dupe, the pompous ass. Every Monday, Wednesday and Thursday — yes. The rest of the week he wanted to do other things, to be another sort of person.

In his home at Blindley Heath the walls of one room were devoted to what could only be described as gems from the philosophers; Kant, Hegel, Russell, Ayer, Descartes were all represented, their thoughts jotted by Tony in a way in which he hoped would one day connect and form one single philosophic whole — the riddle of the universe solved once and for all.

What he didn't see, and I'm sure never saw in the whole of his life, was that the riddle was answered right there in his looking glass. Not a case of 'I think, therefore I am' but 'I am, therefore I think.'

To be Tony Hancock was sufficient for several people's lifetimes. That he couldn't allow his own lifetime to run its natural course is a tragedy. Mercifully there are ample records of his work with Alan and Ray and Denis and Kenneth and Sid and Hattie and Bill and the rest. While the acetate holds out Tony Hancock is going to be with us. Silly, flawed, and infinitely original.

Kenneth Horne — Master Broadcaster

Kenneth Horne was one of a rare breed, the funny upper-class Englishman. The English upper classes are great laughers but rarely (intentionally) inspire laughter. One somehow expects an Irishman or a Scot or a Jew or an American to be amusing but it's hard to think of many well-to-do Englishmen from the home counties who can raise as much as a smile.

Kenneth Horne made people laugh for close on thirty years and was a radio star when radio was the place where stars were made. I first saw him in 1943 when, as the office boy in a music publishers, I had to deliver a musical arrangement to the Fortune Theatre — converted during the war to a BBC recording studio and where programmes were made for the forces overseas. The, to me, god-like figures of Horne, Richard Murdoch and the rest, resplendent in RAF blue, impressed me no end, and I was sorry to leave this mysterious, glamorous world and return to the mundane back room of the publishers and the packing and despatch of sheet music.

I last saw Kenneth Horne in February 1969 on the night he died. I was with him at the Dorchester at an awards function where suddenly and without warning he dropped dead from a massive coronary thrombosis. In the interim I'd met and worked both for and with Kenneth and we had become friends. I don't know why we got on so well together, because we came from quite different backgrounds.

His father was a successful preacher, lecturer and sometime Liberal politician, Silvester Horne. His mother was the Hon. Katherine, and Kenneth was the youngest of seven children. He was known as Curly when young but had lost much of his hair by the time he was in his thirties.

He went briefly to Cambridge and played tennis for the University, but was sent down in 1927 for failure to study. It was the era so piquantly described in Brideshead Revisted, and while Kenneth Horne's failure to apply himself cost him a degree he more than made up for that in the years that followed by hard work and dedication to the business of promoting Triplex Glass. The war gave him the chance to advance from being an amateur entertainer to semi-professional status in partnership with Richard Murdoch, already famous for his collaboration with Arthur Askey in radio's 'Band-Waggon'. Together Wing-Commander Horne and Squadron-Leader Murdoch devised the fictitious RAF station, Much Binding in the Marsh, and made it one of the best known and most loved locales in British radio.

After the war the show continued, but in addition Kenneth Horne was reunited with the world of business, returning to his job at Triplex Glass, then leaving them for the managing directorship of the British Industries Fair, Chad Valley Toys, and Ronuk Floor

Polish. He balanced his show-business and business careers with great skill but at great cost to his health. A stroke almost put him out of action in 1958, but he recovered and from then on concentrated on entertaining.

I first worked for him supplying jokes and so forth when he compèred music hall in the mid-fifties. A writer called Eric Merriman and I devised a half-hour format called 'Beyond Our Ken', which became popular in 1959. In 1960 I left the team and next worked for Kenneth in 1964 on the successor to 'Beyond Our Ken', 'Round The Horne', which I wrote with Marty Feldman, and later Johnnie Mortimer and Brian Cooke. By this time Kenneth and I were firm friends and almost constant companions. Not a day would go by without a phone call, a letter, or a meeting. His energy and humour remained constant and I can remember even on 'bad' days when he found it hard to walk or had some difficulty with his speech, his eyes would twinkle and he'd make some apt remark covering the lapse with a smile. His one vanity was that he hated to be seen wearing spectacles and I (a life-long wearer) had to devise various ruses to persuade him that it was all right to wear specs. Apart from anything else, it enabled him to read the script.

'Round The Horne', which wasn't designed to last, has in fact lingered on and on and can still be heard seventeen years later either in snippets from the three LP's or in full-blooded repeated series. In fact, it is true that every week somewhere in the world someone is listening to 'Round The Horne'. The writing was, and remains, amazingly good to listen to, and the cast were tremendous, but it was Kenneth Horne's triumph; and although in his career as a broadcaster his credits must have run into thousands, I don't think he was ever better than in 'Round The Horne'. More than that, he made everyone he worked with even better. No one who was involved in 'Round The Horne' has ever been funnier — as funny possibly but never funnier — nor has their timing been smoother, or their delivery crisper. Kenneth Horne the super salesman, the benign managing director, the engaging companion, always got the best from anyone he worked with. Like all great leaders he commanded instant loyalty. If you asked any of the thousands of people who worked with Kenneth Horne, both in business and entertainment, what was so remarkable about the man, I'm sure that they would talk of a special relationship that they enjoyed with him. Everyone, that is, except his three wives; for ironically, whilst his public relations flair was phenomenal, his private life seems to have been not much short of disastrous.

This is not to suggest that he was a Jekyll and Hyde; fine with strangers but hell to live with. It's just that I don't think he ever committed himself absolutely to anyone, and no wife likes to be treated like a much-valued and respected employee. Perhaps he was rather naive about people. Like his father, the Liberal orator, perhaps Charles Kenneth Horne loved everyone and found to his dismay that at close quarters on a day-to-day basis too much affection can be stifling. But to write all this is to probe unnecessarily deeply into a man who might have been anything he chose but who was, when all is said and done, just 'a jolly good fellow'. Let his epitaph be then — this decent, good natured man — 'No one was ever nicer'.

Marty

It's difficult to write about a man you know as well as I knew Marty Feldman.

On the one hand there are the good things: the memories of success, of laughter, of shared achievement. On the other there's the truth lurking, like the skeleton beneath the skin, of a man with as many flaws as he had skills. To arrive at even a partial view of the whole man you have to start at the beginning.

Marty was born to a moderately well-to-do Jewish family in London's East End. When he was six years old the war came and Feldman senior departed for the RAF, and Marty and his younger sister, Pamela, were left in the sole charge of their deep-voiced, super-competent mother. Later Marty was sent to a 'Dotheboys Hall' sort of boarding school, and his loathing for the food they served there was the start of a lifelong adherence to vegetarianism. Around this time the family changed its name — from what I don't remember — to Feldman, a change which upset the sensitive Marty. It seemed to him like the loss of identity. Later came the bourgeois family home in north Finchley, and time spent at a sedate north London grammar school, which contrived to push the young Martin Alan Feldman into the tame kind of rebellion that was commonplace among middle-class youths in the late forties and early fifties. A touch of jazz clubs, a hint of drinking in sleazy west end bars and clubs — in one, the Mandrake, Marty met his wife-to-be, Lauretta — a whiff, in short, of Bohemia. Then it was supposed that the young man having sown a wild oat or two would go into his father's business . . . Marty didn't. His father, a dapper, manicured, twinkling-eyed gown manufacturer with a line of amusing, gently-dismissive patter which his son inherited, and whom I first met in the early fifties, would phone me from time to time and ask plaintively, 'Where's Marty?' I didn't know and said so.

Later, when Marty married the Miss Sullivan he'd met at the Mandrake (a soundalike of his mother, psychoanalysts might note, but, unlike his mother, a Catholic from Ireland via south Wales and described by the rest of the Feldman family, she told me at the time, as 'that whore') there were all kinds of uneasinesses until Marty and Lauretta were obviously settled and Marty was prosperous. Me, as the non-Jewish best friend, helped a little to re-cement family ties but mostly it was a natural desire of a loving family to stay intact. So Lauretta became 'okay' and Marty was richer by the hour and all was well.

We wrote together for ten years and at a prodigious speed. A half-hour radio show took us less than two full days and we could write twenty-four and a half minutes' comedy for commercial television in a day. There were, of course, days, weeks even, when we couldn't produce anything at all — we'd temporarily written ourselves out. There were times too when we disagreed over *what* to write but these occasions were rare.

Marty tended to become obsessed with the 'how' of writing. At one period he thought research was essential and however brief the piece we were writing he'd insist that we must visit the British Museum or Madame Tussaud's just to get the picture firmly in our minds of what hieroglyphics actually looked like or to see how Clement Atlee differed from Winston Churchill physically. The fact that you could get the information from a book close at hand wasn't enough. Strangely, this detailed research was never the slightest use for the current project but got used later on for something quite different. Another obsession he had was for quotations, and for a period our characters were forever spouting Shakespeare or Proust or the Bible.

Mainly, though, we used our wits and the work flowed. Together we wrote for Frankie Howerd, Bernard Braden, Jimmy Edwards, Dick Bentley and June Whitfield in 'Take It From Here', Terry Scott, Peter Jones, Harry Worth, Irene Handl, Alfie Bass, Bill Fraser, Clive Dunn, and many more. We wrote a number of sketches for the Ned

51

Sherrin satire shows, and for Felix Aylmer and Hugh Griffiths in a series called 'The Walrus And The Carpenter'. We wrote for radio and television and films, and our writing partnership ended only when we found that we'd started repeating ourselves.

I suppose our most successful work was for Kenneth Horne, Kenneth Williams, Hugh Paddick, Betty Marsden, and Bill Pertwee in 'Round The Horne'. We approached it reluctantly but soon came to enjoy it immensely. We never took it seriously and regarded it as an enormous romp. We hurled the show at the listeners' heads to see if they'd catch it or duck. Most of them caught it and it played to a comfortable eight million people and more a week in the UK, and was sold all over the English-speaking world.

It was highly charged with emotion. Characters were always offering to rip the lid off, to tell all, to confess to nameless sins. The BBC censors became gripped by a revivalist fervour whilst attempting to purify the programme titles — 'We ought to do something about Take Your Partners. Who are they fooling, Take your partners for what?'

In his early manifestations, the walking slum J. Peasemold Gruntfuttock was guided by voices, a sort of Rowton House version of Joan of Arc whose great aim in life was to set fire to things, not least of all himself. Most of our characters had a destructive streak but, and it's a big but, they were self-destructive. Nobody was ever hurt and, looking back, I can see that we had spotted the self-destructive elements in British society at that time and invented our strange gallery of oddities to express what we felt was true of society as a whole.

'Round The Horne' was written at a time when you've never had it so good was wearing just a little thin. 'I'm Backing Britain' didn't seem much more relevant than 'Hang the Kaiser'. The commonplaces of the day were mods and rockers, flower power, the Beatles and Carnaby Street, the musical *Hair*, the Wolfenden Report, the abolition of stage censorship, 'Till Death Us Do Part', and 'TW3'. There was at that time a whole loosening of public and private behaviour. By echoing what was all around us we found ourselves absolutely in tune with our time and the show, because of this, became extraordinarily popular.

Marty and I never got bored with the show for the simple reason that if we did find an idea becoming tedious we'd drop it — often in mid-sentence. 'At this point we were to have heard *The Three Musketeers*, part III but the writers got fed up with it so instead here is a story of darkest Africa as Armpit Theatre presents *Lipharvest of the River*.'

Another element that gave 'Round The Horne' its special quality was the constant change of direction. Working on the principle that the listeners' minds would wander, we allowed our minds to wander too. Side issues would constantly crop up in the sketches — a spy story would suddenly become an out-of-touch impersonator's cabaret act. If we noticed that one of the cast hadn't spoken for a couple of pages his next speech would be a complaint that he hadn't spoken for a while and there'd be rumbles of mutiny from the cast. We noted our own shortcomings as writers. If we couldn't think of anything we'd say so and get out the best way we could.

Because our listeners quickly got to understand that this was what the show *was* they felt allowed in, able to join the conspiracy and consequently their pleasure was enhanced. It's nice to be a member of a club, even if the membership is over eight million people. Good jokes were cheered, bad jokes booed and there were plenty of both. We'd put in anything we thought was funny. We invented a character called Sir Reginald Sweet of the Football Association so that he could answer the phone by saying 'Hello, Sweet F.A.' In another script we had a headless horseman who manifested himself at midnight for a gallop over the moors. Alas, his horse was headless too. They were 'just not equipped for the job'.

Literary pastiche, name dropping, obscure references to current show-business gossip, catalogues of mythical forthcoming events, 'The washroom attendants' flannel dance and zabaglione show will be held in the coal shed at Lord's.' The splendid 'Over eighties nudist leapfrog team', Rambling Syd Rumpo with his private language, Julian and Sandy with theirs. The show, as we caused Kenneth Horne to say on one occasion, was like 'spending thirty minutes in a spin dryer'.

The scripts were full of other meanings but I don't think they were ever dirty. They were rude and often vulgar and, of course, some people objected but the atmosphere that comes through when *I* read the scripts again all these years later is that it was a great lark.

After we'd written fifty shows Marty's career as a performer started to take off and in no time at all he had become a star. He developed what he described to me years later as 'the mania'. A belief that he was not just good, but somehow blessed by the Almighty (a common disease among comedy performers) and he

53

prospered and went to Hollywood and worked for Mel Brooks and then with Gene Wilder, and finally negotiated a six-picture deal with Universal where he wrote, directed and starred in his own films. He asked me to join him in this venture but I declined. I had too many obligations of my own to fulfil in Great Britain. His first picture, *The Last Remake Of Beau Geste*, was pretty grim, his second and last, *In God We Trust,* was a total flop.

And Marty went to Mexico (for a small role in *Yellowbeard the Pirate*), and died there. He had burned himself out. He'd been a great companion and a slippery customer; a brave, joyous iconoclastic rascal and a pain in the neck. I hope there *is* a heaven. When I get there Marty will greet me and say, 'Hey, love, terrific. Now — er . . . I've got this six-picture deal with St Peter . . . why don't we . . . put it together — like we did when we were *alive.*'

The Sublime Peter Sellers

For the first hour the Peter Sellers film, *Revenge Of The Pink Panther*, is as funny as you could wish with Sellers as the monumentally dumb Inspector Clouseau pitching the gags with the skill of a fine spin bowler unerringly finding his mark every time. Later it tends to drag when the plot, an ado about dope smugglers in Hong Kong and Kowloon, tends to stifle mirth, but an hour of wall-to-wall laughter is good going for a comedy these days, and for that hour the going is very good indeed. Mercifully it isn't a very tasteful film and Blake Edwards, who is the master of the big knockabout jokes, sets up a heavy barrage of sight gags that explode (often literally) on to the screen.

The costumiers where the inept Inspector goes for his disguises is called Balls and Co. Togged down as Toulouse Lautrec he is singing 'Thank heaven for little girls . . .' when a bomb — or rather a 'boem' destroys the shop. When the still smouldering Clouseau reports to his superior he sets fire to a document, the document ignites the desk and the Police HQ becomes a towering inferno. Incidentally, Clouseau ascribes his miraculous escape from the holocaust at the costumiers to being sheltered by a consignment of 'inflatable goitres'. As I say, there's not too much good taste around. What there is is Edwards' and Sellers' capacity for being gorgeously destructive. Fourposter beds collapse, people fall into vats of paint and cement, villains plunge through three apartments before being flattened. Cars are machine-gunned and explode in a mass of flames. So violent is it at one point that were it not for Sellers' disarming air of profoundly dignified stupidity you'd freeze at the callousness of it all.

As it is, Sellers as a priest, a barrage-balloon-sized 'Godfather', and best of all as a Swedish sailor, complete with peg-leg and rubber inflatable parrot (which springs a leak and requires repeated energetic pumping to keep it recognizable) is so divinely funny, I for one forgive the film any lapses it might have.

Woody and Annie

My favourite funny man on earth is Woody Allen. He's an amazingly inventive writer and he makes good films. My admiration for him is boundless. Woody Allen is not unlike Lawrence Durrell or, come to that, Dickens in the way he weaves autobiographical material into his work. Like Durrell's *Alexandria Quarter*, Allen's films use the same landscape of the mind over and over, only changing the locale from opus to opus but keeping essentially to the same theme: distrait man unable to make sense of the cosmos but cruelly given enough sense to see his limitations.

Annie Hall is set in contemporary New York and Hollywood, although that's immaterial. All Allen's films take place in his mind, and leap from there via the screen into the audience's lap where they cuddle up and look appealingly at you as if to say 'you understand — don't you?' In *Annie Hall* he takes a more direct route to the audience, occasionally talking to the audience from the screen as Groucho Marx used to do. Allen quotes Groucho's famous 'I wouldn't join a club that would have me as a member' but attributes its source to Freud's book, *Wit And Its Relation To The Unconscious*. And Woody Allen should know. His almost permanent psychoanalysis is as much a hallmark (no pun intended) as Jimmy Durante's nose or Buster Keaton's deadpan.

Annie Hall is subtitled A Nervous Romance — and nervous (or rather, edgy) it is. Annie Hall, played by Diane Keaton in various types of dither, feels inadequate because of her lack of intellect and inability to make love unless relaxed by marijuana or valium. When she's persuaded by Alvy Siner (Woody Allen) to go to a psychiatrist she is at last able to overcome her fears and, newly released from stress, leaves New York for Hollywood to pursue her career as a singer.

With all films that set out to be funny you have to ask — is it? The answer is an unequivocal yes. Woody Allen killing a spider in the bath with a tennis racquet is as splendid a moment as you would wish to see, and his agonized face as he rides as passenger in a car whose driver has confessed not long before to a neurotic desire to drive headlong into the oncoming traffic, is piquant beyond words. Most of Allen's jokes are wordy. After a great moment in bed, he sighs, 'As Balzac would say, there goes another novel.' And 'I've never had so much fun without laughing.' He chides Annie, 'You hear a couple of moths behind the screen and you think it's the Manson family.' A live lobster escapes and scuttles behind the refrigerator. How to get it out? Allen suggests putting a dish of melted butter and a pair of nutcrackers down on the floor.

Woody Allen, more than any other contemporary film maker, has absorbed what our condition is and reveals it to us in a way that's truthful, observant and optimistic. Not that he's slushy. As they drive through Beverly Hills, Annie comments that in comparison to New York it's so clean. Woody Allen, who is kidding nobody that he's a character called Alvy Singer, comments acidly, 'They don't throw away their garbage here. They turn it into TV shows.'

Those fifteen years of psychoanalysis are really paying off — and, as analysts will tell you, 'It's not only the patient we help, it's the people around them.' We, the people around Woody Allen, are definitely scoring. *Annie Hall* is his best film so far and although the one-man band principle can be patchy and often wearisome, Allen has become film by film more assured, confident and stylish. He is a good comic and as such (hangups and all) he should be revered above statesmen, soldiers and priests. After all, when did we last have a Pope who played jazz clarinet?

Obit I — Groucho

The death of Groucho on 22 September 1977 was bound to stimulate a flock of Marx Brothers 'seasons' and The British Academy of Film and Television Arts pushed the boat out with a special screening of *Animal Crackers* as a tribute to Groucho.

Animal Crackers is the one with Captain Spaulding, the African explorer ('I shot an elephant in my pyjamas — what it was doing there I shall never know'), and Chico and Harpo doing the routine where when Chico asks for a flashlight he is offered in turn a flute, a fish, a flit-spray, a hip-flask, and the opportunity to pinch Harpo's cheek. 'Not flesh — flash.' *You* remember. Margaret Dumont is in it too, a performance as superb today as it was in 1930 when the film was made. I'm unrepentant about my feelings towards Marx Brothers films — they are slapdash in the extreme and often wilfully unfunny — but then there's Harpo maniacally trying to break a woman's arm and you forget the tosh as the tears of laughter stream. Oh, if only the Marx Brothers had got together with Mel Brooks! That would have been something to see.

Obit II — Charlie Chaplin

When Sir Charles Chaplin died on Christmas Day 1977 it was almost as if it was an afterthought. He slipped out of the world as unobtrusively as he'd lived in it for the past twenty years: quietly, in Switzerland. In his life he'd been loved and loathed, fêted and vilified, subject to violent abuse and praise that verged on deification. A contemporary of Henry Ford and Pierpoint Morgan, of Hitler and Mussolini, Stalin, Churchill, Roosevelt, Mao Tse-Tung and General Franco, he was more famous and better liked than any of them and survived them all. Indeed Chaplin will survive as long as film survives and will be making people laugh through whatever eternity awaits the human race.

He came into films before anyone really knew how to make them, and left the world at a time when all but a handful had forgotten. In between he made half a dozen great films, many good films and a few stinkers. In recent years it became fashionable among the reach-me-down pundits who scrape a living from the rim of show business to compare Chaplin with Keaton, to Chaplin's detriment, which is as pointless as arguing about who won the battle of Jutland. In *Limelight* the two masters played a short scene together with such harmony and timing that you held your breath, never wanting the scene to end.

When someone is great, comparison is irrelevant; and Chaplin was a great comedian. Not only that; he was a great teacher. His tragedy was that so few bothered to learn. Vic Oliver, the Austrian comedian, used in his act to play a few notes on his violin, stop and say, 'All the great musicians are dead. Beethoven is dead, Brahms is dead, Mozart is dead . . . I'm not feeling too good myself.' With the passing of Chaplin you get a sneaking feeling that all the great English film comedians are dead. Peter Sellers is dead. Stan Laurel is long gone although his films are always with us. Hancock and Sid Field died before they could develop. George Formby, Arthur Lucan and Will Hay were too idiosyncratic to do well in world cinema. Who's left? Well, there's Terry Thomas, but he's settled for character cameos and partial retirement. Peter Ustinov is more of a raconteur than anything else. Dudley Moore *is* a star and so are the Monty Python team as a group. Michael Palin and John Cleese are heading for stardom on their own, and I have a feeling that Cleese is going to be the next really *big* English comedy film star. He is intensely individual, extremely clever and extremely funny. He's already accepted as a television star in England and is sufficiently experienced in film making to be able to make the jump from television to film (and it's a big one: if you don't believe me, ask Morecambe and Wise or Charlie Drake) and determined enough to make sure that things are done his way. Let's face it, the man is obsessed and in the long run it's obsession that makes stars.

Where would Chaplin have been without obsession or Garbo or John Wayne or Hitchcock? Obsession doesn't mean mania, although it hovers close by. Obsession is the overriding conviction that you are right. Cleese has one other quality that makes him an ideal hero in contemporary society. His work totally lacks sentiment. Not for him the tear behind the smile, the hint of tragedy behind the belly laugh. What lies behind Cleese's humour is more sinister. You feel that there may be a razor blade concealed in that custard pie.

Dick And Ian And Porridge

From 1953 until the present day there have been fewer than a dozen absolute hit situation comedies on television — critical *and* box office successes. I would consider shows in the class, a super league if you like, to be 'Hancock's Half Hour', 'Steptoe and Son', 'Till Death Us Do Part', 'The Likely Lads', 'Dad's Army', 'Up

Pompeii', 'Bootsie and Snudge', 'Last Of The Summer Wine', and 'Porridge'.

'Porridge' was written, as was 'The Likely Lads', by Dick Clement and Ian La Frenais. Writing partnerships are odd, and many people are curious as to how they work. I *don't* know how, although I spent ten years as half of Feldman and Took, but I know the ingredients must be that the two writers concerned have similar backgrounds and experience but different personalities. In other words both must share interests but respond to those interests in different ways. George S. Kaufman, co-author of such hit shows as *The Man Who Came To Dinner, You Can't Take It With You, George Washington Slept Here, Dinner At 8*, and *The Solid Gold Cadillac*, was once asked why he collaborated with other writers so often. He said, 'It's nice to have company when you come face to face with a blank page.'

Dick Clement and Ian La Frenais have never considered *why* they collaborate — they just do. If pressed, Dick will admit that when you write in partnership the rewrites get done as you go along, which saves a lot of time in rehearsal. But writing partnerships can produce a lot of strain. Do they never argue? 'Never,' says La Fenais — and it's difficult to imagine them falling out. They're two calm, balanced, imaginative men with a great deal of success and a string of writing awards behind them. I interviewed them just before the hit series 'Porridge' started. In case you missed it, 'Porridge' was set in prison and Ronnie Barker played an old lag doing time yet again, and if not exactly beating the system at least surviving the horrors and humiliations of the nick without crumbling into apathetic dust.

Why prison?

'We've always wanted to write a comedy about two men stuck in a lift,' says Ian. I suppose that a prison cell is like that, confined, intimate yet impersonal — on the way to somewhere else. I reminded them that Ray Galton and Alan Simpson had written a 'Hancock's Half Hour' about a group of people stuck in a lift and Dick and Ian started to rhapsodize over Hancock. 'Do you remember that wonderful show that starts with Tony saying "I'm bored" and spends thirty minutes discussing the idea of boredom?' 'What about "Steptoe". All that depth with just two men in a room — brilliant!'

Clement and La Frenais sit back and stare into space for a moment, each considering the possibilities of nothingness, then both together they rush back into speech filling the vacuum with their thoughts and ideas, laughing at each other's inventiveness, clowning as they order lunch, warm and together in a potentially hostile world. Not that Burke's where we were lunching, is particularly hostile. It's a West End waterhole for upper-echelon show-business people, actors, writers, the handful of survivors from what was once the film industry. Dick and Ian are treated with great deference. They're regular customers, and successful too. What more could any restaurant wish? As we wait for the food to arrive, the conversation roams around show-business topics.

Wasn't 'The Family' incredible. The mother was great . . . and what about the next-door neighbour who came in and started talking about sex? Ian ad libs a chunk of dialogue — '. . . and he always says thank you.' They laugh — not maliciously but with genuine admiration for the series and what it revealed. You get the feeling that if there had been no 'Family' they'd have invented it.

Dick and Ian started their writing career with a hit, 'The Likely Lads'. It had been Dick's production exercise when he was a trainee director and its quality was immediately apparent. It quickly became popular. James Bolam and Rodney Bewes became stars. Dick moved on to direct Peter Cook and Dudley Moore in 'Not Only But Also'. Ian wrote plays on his own. Together they wrote films, which Dick directed. Then with the film industry in disarray Dick and Ian dropped out of the limelight. They were still writing for the cinema but somehow the films weren't getting made. *Nobody's* films were getting made.

Their return to the small screen with 'Whatever Became Of The Likely Lads' put them straight back to the top of the writing tree, their work if anything better than before.

Ian says, 'When we were doing the research for "Porridge" we spent a day in Brixton Prison going through the routine of admission. God, it was traumatic. There's just no privacy . . . It's claustrophobic . . . Hell.' Dick joins in — 'We came out thinking how can we be funny about this, but then we thought, they're surviving. Let's write about survival.'

I note a common factor in Dick Clement's and Ian La Frenais's work — they don't agree but I press on anyway. 'Thick as Thieves', 'Likely Lads', 'Porridge' — they're all about being trapped. The marriage trap, the friendship trap, the prison trap. Maybe like the man who to his amazement realized that he'd been speaking prose all his life — perhaps all their working lives they've been writing about two men trapped in a lift. Themselves.

Susan Harris — The Woman Behind 'Soap'

Having written slightingly about soap operas myself I suppose I should have been more enthusiastic when the American parodies 'Mary Hartman Mary Hartman', and 'Soap' eventually appeared. It seemed to me, though, that they fell into the very traps they were parodying — the constant repetitious catchphrases, clichéd characters and stories with just enough plot to stop them turning to stone. It was, however, interesting to meet Susan Harris.

On first sight she looks more like one of the stars of 'Charlie's Angels' than the creator, writer and producer of the hotly controversial American television comedy, 'Soap'.

The leggy redhead (a hint of Marti Caine in the face), who could be taken for Goldie Hawn's brighter sister, is a serious person and claims to be dedicated to the possibility of raising the level of television comedy. For that, if for nothing else, Susan Harris deserves the Broadcasting Press Guild award for the 'best imported programme', which she flew into London to collect in 1980. To Susan Harris, 'Good comedy can be very, very serious. It contains elements of tragedy,' and 'Soap' certainly does that.

The story of how Susan Harris came into television writing has a fictional ring to it. Divorced, with a two-year-old son to support, she was watching television and thought, 'This is garbage. I can do better,' and sat down and wrote a script. It was accepted. 'It seemed fairly simple,' she says. 'All you have to do is make people talk.'

After the experience of writing episodes of 'All In The Family', and 'Maude', both American spin-offs of the British 'Till Death Us Do Part', she created a partly autobiographical series about a divorced woman, 'Fay', and then came 'Soap'.

'Soap', in fact, was only the working title and she says, 'I was too lazy to change it.' But it was accepted by one of the three big American networks, ABC, and a pilot show was made. Before it hit the air word got out that 'Soap' was to contain scenes of explicit sex, and deal with adultery, homosexuality, murder, impotence and many other taboo subjects, not in a serious way but strictly for laughs.

61

Like Monty Python's *Life Of Brian*, these rumours roused a storm of protest from religious groups, none of whom had seen the show, and it was touch and go whether the series would ever see the light of day. But the network stood firm, the series became popular and three years on the only mail that Susan Harris had received was of thanks and congratulations.

The secret, of course, is how these subjects are treated, and Susan Harris has a shrewd touch in skirting the danger area or tackling it in a way that is at once thoughtful and sensitive. Thanks to a superb cast (incidentally, the largest in any US television series), the stories seem so natural and unforced that, as with 'The Archers', you really believe in these people and their problems. The Tates and the Campbells may not be like *us* but they're like people we know. Like a good cook, Susan Harris has a light touch with her concoctions, and you never feel jaded by too much repetition.

A serious woman with a humorous streak, she writes to please herself and admits that occasionally one strand or another of the continuing story doesn't work. The Martian sequence where Burt was replaced by a priapic lookalike she thinks now may have been a mistake, but Chuck and Bob, the schizophrenic ventriloquist and his dummy who could have been a disaster have, in fact, proved very popular.

The success of 'Soap' worldwide pleases her immensely, but I asked her if the change of language affected the humour. She said, 'I don't think so. I've seen it in Japanese and it's hilarious.'

Susan Harris is pragmatic, gifted and alert, and by a long way the best-looking script writer I've ever met. She doesn't watch a lot of television, agreeing with Woody Allen that in Hollywood garbage is turned into television shows rather than thrown away, but she's proud of 'Soap', which indeed has blown like a breath of fresh air through the dusty cliché-ridden corridors of television comedy. This genuine housewife-superstar has her feet planted firmly on the ground. 'The truth is,' she says, 'I write out of fear.' A very remarkable lady.

Alan Whicker

I must confess an enormous liking for Alan Whicker. He laughs easily and enjoys life. He's richer than most of us but never leaves you with the feeling that you are poorer. He's inquisitive without being impertinent, and takes people at their own valuation, and places as they are. He seems always to ask the question you would have liked to ask yourself and to be in the spot, whether Alaska, Miami or Patagonia, that seems, when he's there at any rate, to be amazingly interesting. He is, in short, the perfect television travelling man, strutting jauntily into each new situation with the assurance of a punter going up to the tote window with a fistful of winning tickets. Alan Whicker has always been a loner. In the days when most leading journalists did time on *Picture Post*, Whicker kept to the other side of the street working for *Men Only*. When the Baverstock/Milne revolution turned early evening television into the time you watched 'Tonight', Whicker joined the team, but, as always, flew solo.

In 1978 he went to India and returned with a two-hour film about Bombay: 'Don't Feel Guilty About Your Cadillac — And I Won't Feel Guilty About My Bicycle'. As always the apt phrases clinked like ice in a tumbler. In a city where a million people sleep in the street and millions more fester in the appalling squalor of the shanty towns that hug the giant luxury apartment blocks, Whicker commented that it was 'as if chaos has triumphed over reason'. Walking through the teeming nightmare of human degradation his feeling of 'being walled in by people' reinforced the images of 'horror, disgust, grief and hopelessness'. In a rare moment of understatement he described his visit to Bombay as 'a disconcerting experience'.

The programme wasn't all about beggars and despair. An Indian princess talked at length about a society ordered by God, of reincarnation and fatalism. But then it's easy to talk about the natural order of things when you're on top of the heap.

For many the only escape is in the cinema. In India six million people a day go to the movies, which were described by the charmingly outspoken lady editor of a fan magazine as 'mindless banality . . . 99 per cent awful.' She talked with dainty cynicism of the slow dawning of permissiveness in the Indian cinema and the first screen kiss, the prospect of which had the crowds queueing for days. She saw the emerging Indian sex symbol as being 'a cross between Christine Keeler and (long pause) . . . Princess Anne.'

63

The dauntless Alan took it all with raised eyebrows and a chuckle of disbelief. He was more deadpan with a group of Brits, lingering remnants of an Empire long gone, who mourned in accents of an upper classness no longer to be heard in England the passing of the dinner jacket and the 'boiled shirt'. It can't be easy to describe, and virtually impossible to explain, a country where a film star can earn a million pounds a year 'easily' but where millions earn nothing at all. That Whicker's programme on India nearly did, it was a near miracle and proves, if proof were needed, that although he is much imitated he has never been surpassed.

Raymond Briggs

When you look at Raymond Briggs's drawings and the simple narrative connecting them, it's easy at first glance to dismiss his work as pleasant but uncomplicated; accessible and undemanding. Reminiscent, possibly, of Edward Ardizzone, you think. Then you look again and see the sprightliness and the unsnobbishness, and you become aware that the drawing is doing a heck of a lot of work in its discreet way and that the occasional speech bubble is all you need. Indeed in *The Snowman*, which he created in 1978, Briggs disposes of bubbles altogether and lets the action tell the story of the snowman who comes to life and spends the night amazed and delighted in the new-found world of 'indoors', his guide and mentor the small boy who built him. In return he takes the child on a literally flying visit to Brighton, and with Briggs you feel his characters are on the move. Whether it's the snowman lowering himself blissfully into a deep freeze as we might ease ourselves into a hot bath, or the small boy demonstrating his skateboard, the sense of movement is vivid. The posture of the boy's body, though the skateboard is still, tensely indicative of the stance of the expert skateboarder in action, is perfect.

Raymond Briggs's *Father Christmas* dates from 1973, but the details of the rubicund old buffer's home — outside lavatory, kitchen sink — date unashamedly from forty years earlier, a time when false teeth could be found in a glass on the bamboo bedside table. Father Christmas's gas stove, kettle, teapot, and the paraphernalia of breakfast remind me strongly of my childhood in the thirties — and no doubt of Briggs's too. He was born in 1934, the year that Hitler became Führer, and Shostakovitch wrote his opera *Lady Macbeth Of Mzensk* — the one that Stalin found embarrassing and vulgar.

Both subjects could be a suitable case for treatment by Briggs, as he has a taste for the tasteless, which he indulges to the hilt in *Fungus The Bogeyman*. 'Bogeydom', says Briggs, 'is dark, dim, unclean, indefinite, indistinct, abstruse, difficult to understand, unexplained, doubtful, hidden, secluded, remote from public observation, unknown, lowly, humble, dull, dingy, gloomy, murky . . .' In short, it's about sights and sounds and smells that are not normally discussed in polite society but exist, nonetheless, and are the stuff that rude jokes are made of.

Briggs's tale of family life among the Bogeys — a tribe of things who live in a slimelight world under the earth's crust, concerns Fungus, his wife, Mildred, and his son, Mould. Their conversation consists of such pleasantries as 'The Outside lavatory is working again, drear.' (Drear is bogey for dear.) 'I know, Mildred, drearest, I must get it blocked.' And, 'Take care, Fungus, my darkling. Try not to get your feet dry.' As you can tell, it's a matter of simply reversing the norm and then drawing it.

Ah, but if it was as simple as that, many would have done it. For all I know, many *have* attempted it, but no one has worked the trick with such thorough-going skill as Raymond Briggs. *Fungus* is a big seller, and a pop-up, or rather 'plop-up' book outlining his activities is also available for the young in head. The intellectual godparents of *Fungus The Bogeyman* are Aldous Huxley and George Orwell; the former seeing the horrors of a totally sanitized world and the latter the ultimate nastiness in 1984 of Big Brother and the Ministry of Love.

In his tastes, Briggs is fairly traditional, admitting to liking roast beef, Beachcomber, and Fawlty Towers. He also likes reading, gardening, walking, and browsing in second-hand bookshops. So what is it, I wonder, that gives a man who enjoys such pleasantly normal things a liking for the bizarre? Why make the hero of a tale of romantic aspirations a lavatory attendant? Well, Gentleman Jim, the fantasizing loo-keeper, is just that, and I suppose the link between subterranean lavatory and the world of the Bogeys is not hard to find.

Gentleman Jim, in which Briggs slyly reminds us what a good draughtsman he is, follows the spiralling obsessions of the good, simple, credulous Jim, and his trusting wife. Jim finishes up in prison looking after the toilets, an ironic twist in a story that points the moral that to confuse imagination with reality is a dangerous business.

When The Wind Blows also features Jim and his wife and Briggs's well — not obsession perhaps, but — preoccupation with the simplicities of cheerful, simple, working-class life. Jim is now retired and living in the Sussex countryside. As he says, 'My life isn't very fast moving or dynamic,' and, in fact, all the action comes from the outside world. When The Wind Blows is about the nuclear holocaust, and Jim and his wife's preparations for it as prescribed by government handbooks. It is possibly the most chilling indictment of the nuclear arms race that I have ever seen. The chubby, round-faced, simple people of Raymond Briggs's imagination progress from a world where the most important problem is whether to have sausages or beefburgers for lunch to the problems of building a fall-out shelter using doors, cushions and a mattress.

Jim knows what to expect: 'You get triffic heat with these bombs,' he tells his uncomprehending wife; and 'Only the fittest will survive the outcome of the Nuclear Holocaust.' Jim knows the theory of the next war and patiently prepares for it, using his memories of World War II as a guide to what it will be like. 'The Black-out . . . the all clear . . . cups of tea . . . the ARP . . . Old Churchill on the wireless . . . Vera Lynn singing away . . . ITMA . . .' And then the bomb drops and Jim and his wife survive! And their survival is more horrific than if they *had* died. They gradually disintegrate as the fall-out starts to work its sickening evil and quietly and without fuss, brave as simple people are, they accept these new horrors and wait patiently until final, blessed oblivion. When The Wind Blows is a moving book, a horrifying book, a work of great stature from a man who has never shied away from reality. It should be required reading for all politicians and jingoistic 'no-nonsense' militarists. It is a book that though designed for adults should be in every school library and used without emotion (if that is possible) when describing what nuclear war means. It is a book about simple, harmless, decent people being destroyed casually by the most disgusting apparatus designed by man.

Raymond Briggs is a good storyteller, a fine artist, and a dealer in great truths. In When The Wind Blows he has a vision of the future that could not be more sombre. Let's hope that history, just this once, will prove him wrong.

Overheard At The Club

It was Stephen Potter who gave us the word clubmanship, a department of his wider scheme for better living. To be a member of a club — whether golf, squash, croquet or poker — suggests togetherness, conviviality, annual dinners and spring lunches where, if you survive the speeches, the opportunity for a chat over the port with people of a like mind is unrivalled.

In the narrower sense, of course, clubmanship relates to the great establishments in Pall Mall or Duke Street. In such clubs one mingles with statesmen, politicians, newsreaders, the chairmen of television panel games, senior civil servants — in short, the highest in the land.

It was when I was a member of the massively elegant Reform Club that I met and gossiped to one of my great heroes, the American humorist, S. J. Perelman. S. J. is to would-be humorists what St Paul is to would-be clergymen, and actually to meet the man, and a fellow member at that, was as if an aspiring Elizabethan playwright had suddenly found himself at the Mermaid Tavern sharing a flagon with William Shakespeare. Our conversation turned to the discussion of mutual friends. One such was a noted American literary agent and raconteur whom, discretion being after all the hallmark of the Clubman, I had better call X.

Perelman said, 'Did you ever notice that X walked with the rolling gait of a sailor?' I said that I had and had always wondered why. As far as I knew, X had always *flown* the Atlantic. 'Well,' said Perelman, 'it was born of hero worship.' When X was young the man he most admired in all New York was his Uncle Sam, whom the youngster always assumed to be a big man in the world of shipping. Uncle Sam was frequently at sea and after each lengthy absence would return to New York even richer and more elegant than before, his nautical roll being the only thing to pick him out from the ranks of similarly prosperous businessmen, bankers and stockbrokers. 'Was Uncle Sam a shipping magnate?' I asked. 'No,' said Perelman, 'he was a card sharp.' In those days the saloons of ocean-going liners such as the *Mauretania* and the *Aquitania* bore discreet signs which read 'Beware of plausible strangers,' and X's uncle was just such a plausible stranger, willing, indeed anxious, to help well-heeled travellers pass the long hours of the Atlantic crossing with a little poker or cribbage.

And so it was that Uncle Sam, who didn't know his port from his starboard, was in young X's eyes every inch a sailor. 'As time went on, X imitated his uncle in more ways than one,' said S. J. Perelman, 'and in my dealings with him in literary matters I always felt that it would be fitting in the outer office of his suite in Madison Avenue there should be a sign which read "Beware of plausible Literary Agents."'

X's real name? Well it wouldn't be fitting for me to reveal it here, but he became a prominent figure in the 'satire boom' of the sixties making frequent appearances on television in 'TW3' and its successors.

If you really want to know who he was you'll have to ask Ned Sherrin or David Frost, Bernard Levin or Norman St John Stevas . . . they're bound to know the man who talked like a character out of Damon Runyan but walked like someone out of a novel by Joseph Conrad.

Part two

Reviews

Live on Stage

I left the orange peel and red plush of Music Halls for Intimate Revue in 1956. To be precise, a revue called *For Amusement Only*, which opened at the Apollo Theatre in Shaftesbury Avenue on 5 June 1956.

I had arrived there by the simple act of making the authors, Peter Myers and Ronnie Cass, laugh at an audition. So much so that I was called back later that day for a second audition at which the producer was present. I ambled on to the stage, paused and said, 'Act Two, same as Act One.' There was a great deal of laughter — I went into my routine for the second time, and with my music-hall experience behind me warmed to my task and got a big hand.

So, I was *in* and spent three hectic weeks rehearsing with the company which included Ron Moody, Pat Lancaster, and Hugh Paddick (all of whom subsequently featured in the first of the two great Kenneth Horne radio series, 'Beyond Our Ken'), Thelma Ruby and Barbara Young. The ingenue was a lissom seventeen-year-old called Judy Carne who some years later made her name in Hollywood as the 'sock it to me' girl in 'Rowan and Martin's Laugh In'.

This was followed by three weeks on the road, a pause to polish, and then the excitement of a West End first night. Ronnie Stevens stopped the show with his solo number, and so did Jimmy Thompson in an extravagant impersonation of Liberace. In short,

71

the show was a riot and the cheers at the end, augmented by the thundering feet of the Gallery first nighters who showed their delight with rhythmical stamping, let all know in no uncertain terms that *For Amusement Only* was a hit.

It ran for two years, by which time I'd become a regular broadcaster and had appeared in cabaret in such exalted venues as the Grill Room of the Dorchester Hotel in Park Lane, Quaglino's (the favoured night spot of the late Lord Mountbatten) and the Blue Angel — the club in which David Frost was discovered by Ned Sherrin some years later. There were other clubs, too, some owned and frequented by the trendy, some owned, it turned out later, by the underworld.

A second revue in which I had slightly better billing and a shade more money — a successor to *Amusement* and called *For Adults Only* — ran for a year or so at the Strand Theatre before tiptoeing into the night of theatrical history. It had a talented cast including Miriam Karlin, Ron Moody and Hugh Paddick (again), Frederick Jaeger, and Richard Waring. The book was fairly leaden but the skill and talent of the cast kept it afloat until the backers got their money back.

After that I turned to full-time script-writing and the theatre saw me no more. No great loss. When, years later, I became second-string theatre critic for *Punch* and occasional professional theatregoer for Radio 4's 'Kaleidoscope', revue in the old sense was dead, killed forever by *Beyond The Fringe*, the brilliance of which — it was said — could never be equalled. Not everybody believed this and, indeed, *Oh Calcutta*, which was a revue — if only of pudenda — broke box office records. But by and large Intimate Revue was dead, and it was with a feeling of foreboding that in August 1977 I attended the first night of an all-woman revue, *After Shave*.

There Ain't Nobody Here But Us Chicks

The musical revue *After Shave* at the *Apollo* had what I would call a really good, old-fashioned first night. The curtain went up ten minutes behind schedule to allow for latecomers — the programmes were free, the ladies received gifts of small bottles of toilet water, the men likewise. The stalls heaved and moiled with

friends of producer and cast; there were celebrities dotted about —
at least I assume they were celebrities, they wore white suits and
caps and carried golfing umbrellas which is a sure sign of a
celebrity — isn't it? There was rapturous applause at intervals
throughout the show from groups of wellwishers, and occasional
cries of 'Jolly Good' and 'Brilliant' from here and there as ghastly
number followed ghastly number and we who were unacquainted
with the aforementioned producer and cast sat in stricken silence
anxiously counting the number of items still to come and praying
for the end.

Those of us who'd suffered the director Christie Dickason's last
fiasco, *Shoot Up At Elbow Creek*, at the Greenwich Theatre,
greeted each other at the final curtain like survivors of the third
battle of the Somme. According to the programme, Ms Dickason's
special talents include mountain climbing and milking a cow. They
do not appear to include directing a musical revue. Her technique
is simple. Take a cliché and run it into the ground. The five ladies
who make up the cast tend to enter with a crab-like gait, bellow
their words into one of the ten microphones (yes — ten; count them
— ten, not to mention the radio mike for one of the rare items with a
modicum of movement) and exit with the fixed grin of someone
who has just broken wind at a chess tournament.

I won't embarrass the cast further by naming them here — clearly
they had enough trouble on their hands without me adding to it. All
I could find to say was 'what are nice girls like that doing in a mess
like this?' As for the author of the lyrics and what might — at a pinch
— be called sketches, my mother always used to say, 'If you can't
find anything good to say about somebody, don't say anything at
all.' So I won't.

John, Paul, George, Ringo — and Bert

It has been my experience that theatre critics want the show they're
reviewing to be a success. No one writes deliberately bitchy
comments in order to get a cheap laugh, but all too often one's
hopes of a good evening and a chance to write columns of praise
are dashed by the poorness of the writing, the clumsiness of the
acting, or the sheer banality of the idea. In short, better a good
juggler than a bad Hamlet.

73

But when you do spot a newcomer of great talent it's a really thrilling occasion. Such an occasion was the West End opening night of *John, Paul, George, Ringo and Bert.* The newcomer was Barbara Dickson.

The scene is an imagined reunion of the Beatles in a Liverpool concert hall. Centre stage a coffin which holds their guitars. And you think, 'Hang on, we're in for a rough night of symbolism,' but — thank heavens — the threat never materializes.

John, Paul, George and Ringo argue but agree to work together once more 'as long as we don't start *thinking* Beatles again'. Enter Bert, who, like the stage manager in Thornton Wilder's *Our Town,* pops in and out of the action to re-live for our benefit the Beatles Saga. Or, rather, he's like a mundane John the Baptist telling us in retrospect of the coming of the Lord. His own apotheosis comes when he is eventually transformed into a pop star himself.

The real Beatles story is a Grand Guignol affair and the glimpses we have of it in *John, Paul, George, Ringo And Bert* are spine chilling enough. Nothing notable is left out, although it seems to me that a few wives are dropped en route and the boys' mildly disastrous film career is only hinted at but, as Vic Oliver used to say, 'What was left was very good.'

The production is clearly influenced by Joan Littlewood — which is not a bad thing, and although the play is no *Oh What A Lovely War,* it's good to see that perhaps Liverpool has something to learn from London after all.

The surprise of the evening is Barbara Dickson, who plays the piano and sings, which is like saying that Gary Player is a golfer and that Germany has a football team. Miss Dickson sings in a voice of slate and marble, brass and fire. It's the voice of the Liverpool Kop, it's a voice in love with what it sings, a voice made for singing. We see little enough of her during the evening as she sits on stage, but not in the action, belting out the appropriate Lennon/McCartney songs to mark the developing action. It's only during the curtain calls that the audience gets a good look at this large, gawky girl wearing gold-framed spectacles, but when they do they show their appreciation in a way reminiscent of a Liverpool football crowd when Kevin Keegan scores the winning goal.

The author, Willy Russell, is the latest in the line of good English provincial dramatists who write the commonplaces of every-day living into universal themes, and he does it well, with humour and some skill.

The Beatles were always there to be written about and while they existed they *were* written about — constantly. (And still are today.) Willy Russell's achievement is to put them in context, to see them as a part of other people's lives and to make dramatic sense of their odd rise to fame.

Experts on the Beatles abound, but I'm afraid I'm not one of them. I've always thought of the Beatles as amiable young men who sang and wrote pleasant pop music but their cult is clearly still powerful enough for a folklore to exist in which John is hero, Paul is suspect and George and Ringo are clowns. Don't ask me why this is so, but it is. In this mythology, Brian Epstein, their first manager, is equated with the Virgin Mary and Allan Klein is Pontius Pilate.

Robert Stigwood, who worked with Epstein and in fact ran the organisation after Epstein's death, isn't mentioned, but this is probably due to Mr Stigwood's natural shyness, for after all he is one of the co-producers of the play.

There's a point in the action where after early failure, Epstein secures the Beatles a recording contract with Parlophone, a record label they've never heard of. 'Who records for Parlophone?' 'Peter Sellers and Jimmy Shand.' 'God — we'll be bunched together with all the freaks.' A strangely prophetic thing to say.

A Hat Full Of Musicals

I'd like you to know that just lately I've been walking with a new bounce in my step. I whistle a lot. I have taken to singing in lifts (next to bathrooms, lifts have the greatest acoustics for non-singers like me), and generally acting like Richard Tauber in *Lilac Time* — that is to say, badly. Why is it, my friends ask earnestly. Could it be because the sun is out and his lumbago has temporarily abated? No. The answer's simple. I won't have to go to another West End musical for some time.

I have adorned the stalls at many of our leading theatres, drinking in the various delights of such entertainments as *Sweeney Todd, On The Twentieth Century, Evita, Chicago,* and *Annie*. The last three particularly interested me as they'd all been running a year or more, all had had cast changes, and with the alleged cash problems of West End theatres, it seemed a good idea to look at that most costly of theatrical enterprises — the musical.

Well, I'll tell you one reason why they're costly — it's all the scenery. The celebrated director, Harold Prince (*Evita, Sweeney Todd*) has a mania for filling his stages with old iron in a variety of forms. And it doesn't just lie there rusting — it moves. It moves up, down, sideways, backwards, and forwards, making the noise you'd expect old iron to make. When it won't move on its own, it is manhandled on and off the stage by either stagehands dressed as actors or actors acting as stagehands. a rich area for demarcation disputes, I'd have thought, but no matter — Mr Prince is a very important man in the theatre and if he says, 'Fifteen men in mufflers and overcoats will manhandle an iron staircase from upstage right to downstage left,' that's what they're going to do. Mr Prince probably figures that it's art. It is my belief that it's bunk. I cannot believe, and God knows I'll believe almost anything, that there was no other way of staging Evita than by filling the stage of the Prince Edward Theatre with what looks like a false start to the Industrial Revolution.

Mercifully, the show overwhelms the scenery and with Marti Webb as Eva (except, said my programme, 'at certain performances' when the part is taken by Stephanie Lawrence) and the estimable Mark Ryan as Che, the piece fairly rattled the polyglot London summer audience into wild and enthusiastic applause. What fun a Japanese tourist can find in a musical about Eva Peron, which at best is about sixty per cent audible, I'll leave for you to conjecture, but *Evita* is clearly the show foreign visitors wish to see, and I sat waiting for the curtain to rise at the Prince Edward Theatre and didn't hear a single English voice.

Admittedly, at the performance of *Chicago* at the Cambridge Theatre that I attended, there was a loquacious American gentleman from Miami who delighted, or at least informed, those within earshot (most of the stalls) with the pertinent details of the cost of visiting Europe, but *Chicago* fairly soon silenced even him. It's noisy, is *Chicago*, and brash and moderately tuneful but, alas, not long for the West End. It's a musical version of the old Ginger Rogers movie, *Roxie Hart*, and tells of the varying publicity values in twenties newspaper of assorted mureteresses.

Here, as with *Evita*, much of the cast had changed since it opened and in the version of *Company* I saw, I commend to you Jacqui Toye as Roxie's rival in homicide, Velma Kelly, and Erick

Ray Evans in an assortment of roles ranging from cop to judge, with much in between. They both played with skill, judgement and flair and it's my hope that on someone's drawing-board somewhere is a play that will project them both into the big time. They deserve it.

Of all the musical plays I saw, the most enjoyed was undoubtedly *Annie*. I say enjoyed, meaning enjoyed by the audience. It's all very well for a critic to say, 'I laughed till my sides ached,' or 'This will run and run,' but it's the people who pay to be entertained who count, and the cash customers *loved* it, and to be honest I did too. It's neat and bright and fresh and so well disciplined are the cast and so alert the management that it appeared to be as crisp as when it opened more than two years earlier in May 1978.

Here again the cast had changed since opening night. Charles West played Daddy Warbucks, Catherine Monte played Annie, and Stella Moray was Miss Hannigan, the tipsy, sluttish matron of the orphanage. Miss Moray brought a loony magic to her far from easy part. One moment the awful custodian of Annie and her fellow orphans, the next a heartwarmingly baleful paedophobe — her performance was a brilliant mixture of pantomime dame, Ethel Merman and Fernandel, and if you had the time, the money and a child to take to the theatre, then I recommend that that theatre should be the Victoria Palace, and the show *Annie*. I couldn't remember when I'd enjoyed an evening in the theatre more. And there wasn't a stagehand in sight.

There's magic and delight about good musical theatre but it strikes me that when the emphasis is on production and not on content there's possibly something missing from the content. I believe that action is the province of the actors, not the scenery. After all, when did you last encore a scrap-yard?

Hello Carol — Goodbye Dolly

I had to report the return in 1979 of *Hello Dolly* to the Theatre Royal, Drury Lane, more in sorrow than in anger. I'd always managed to miss the show up to then, both in the theatre and the cinema, so I couldn't complain. But when it did finally catch up with me I must confess that I found it a load of catchpenny nonsense. Admittedly there are a couple of good songs, 'It Only Takes A Moment', and

'So Long Dearie', and it could be said with truth that Carol Channing gave a super-star performance. Miss Channing, her nose like a freshly chalked billiard cue and with enough cheek to be a strong contender for the presidency of the United States, carried us through the evening gently as with backward children to the ecstasies of applause at the final curtain. As to the piece itself, *Hello Dolly* is the nearest thing I've seen to *Springtime For Hitler*, the shock-horror-success musical in the film *The Producers*. Based on Thornton Wilder's *The Matchmaker*, it tells of a turn-of-the-century marriage arranger whose mission in life is, she says, 'to meddle'. Well, theoretically, it tells the story but it's a musical so sense gets forgotten pretty soon and we are, in theory at least, carried away to a never-never land on the enchanted wings of song. The first-night audience *were* carried away (unless, of course, they were lying) and managed to applaud and cheer the most banal, trivial and inept moments of a production that looked as ancient as the original story. It is my considered opinion that *that* audience would have applauded a coronary thrombosis, the sinking of the *Titanic*, or the start of World War III.

Among the dross of a presentation that appears to owe a lot to Westworld and where for long stretches I really did consider the possibility that we were watching a troupe of extremely sophisticated androids, Eddie Braken shone. His voice mellowed to a nice blend of W. C. Fields and James Stewart, he moved through the action with practised ease. Having once upon a time co-starred with Betty Hutton, I imagine he can cope with anything, even a leading lady so heavily 'miked' you could hear her lightest whisper clear across Covent Garden.

For the rest, energy took the place of ingenuity and the cast was drilled to Brigade of Guards standard. The trouble was that in the process somebody or other had forgotten that the point of the exercise is to enchant us.

Waiting For Colin

Alan Coren and I have a silly bet that in three hundred years Tom Stoppard will be forgotten and Harold Pinter will still be played. Coren's money is on Stoppard, but to me the more neatly tailored information a playwright gives you the less interested you become in the play. A good play makes you wonder at it — in short, it makes you work. It's the mystery of Shakespeare that makes him more appealing than the intellectual Bernard Shaw, and the same goes, to my mind, for the puzzling Pinter versus the witty, game-playing Stoppard.

With Alan Ayckbourn it's a different case. He is the late twentieth-century version of Wedekind, or perhaps Ben Travers, although, of course, in the 1970s Travers and Ayckbourn had plays on in London at the same time. The thing that shines out of Ayckbourn's plays is not the intellect but the craftsmanship. Finely honed in Scarborough, they arrive in the West End in very good shape — the problem is, it seemed to me after several doses of Ayckbourn (I particularly liked *The Norman Conquests*) you begin to see similarities and notice that they all have the *same* shape and much the same content.

In 1975 I was spending most of my evenings in the theatre whilst during the day I was adapting Stephen Potter's *Oneupmanship* for the small screen. Richard Briers starred in the tv series, and the association was the start of a friendship which has continued to this day. When I had to review him in Ayckbourn's play at the Garrick Theatre I had mixed feelings. After all if the play was rotten and I panned it what would I say to him in the studio the following day?

The play he was in, *Absent Friends,* was nothing special, but thankfully Briers was brilliant.

Absent Friends was Alan Ayckbourn's tenth play to be presented in the West End and although I haven't seen them all, I'm beginning to grasp the Ayckbourn formula. Six people roughly coupled are put into a middle-class situation and invited to extricate themselves as best they can. There's the *success* — Peter Bowles in this case; his *wife,* Pat Heywood here (Sheila Hancock in *Absurd Person Singular,* and Penelope Keith in *The Norman Conquests*) who has some sort of nervous breakdown someway into the action; a pair of *indifferent lovers* — indifferent to each other that is; a *loner,* here skilfully done by Phyllida Law, and a *disruptive influence.* That's the part Tom Courtenay had in *Norman Conquests* and Robert Morley played in *How The Other Half Loves.* Richard Briers played it in *Absurd Person Singular,* and did it again with variations in *Absent Friends.*

He played Colin, a chum departed from the bosom of a group of friends and not missed all that much, who — having suffered the

79

tragic loss of his girlfriend by drowning — was about to re-enter their lives via a Saturday tea at the home of Diana and Paul. The other members of the cast awaited his coming with a drizzle of conversation sparsely populated with jokes: 'Where are you going?' 'To the lavatory,' and in due course (forty-two minutes by my watch) he arrived. That was the moment you thank whoever you pray to that Colin was played by Richard Briers. A wink, a snort, a word, a pause, a grin and suddenly you're watching a comedy.

He talked about his dead fiancée, showed holiday snaps of her, pontificated, bored the pants off those assembled but mercifully not off the audience, and went — leaving things as they had been when he arrived.

Well, you're thinking, *that* doesn't sound like much of a play, and it wasn't. It's like a sixth carbon copy of *The Norman Conquests* and even on opening night it felt as if it had been running for ten years — but then I suppose it *had* under one title or another.

After that review, I was surprised that Richard Briers was quite cross with me for being lukewarm about the play. 'It's my living, old boy,' he pointed out.

'Well, writing about it is mine,' I riposted.

Ah, but then no actor really likes critics. They see too much and, of course, an uncomfortable seat, a poor eyeline, or an over-vigorous claque on the first night, makes the critic cross and he tends to take out his ire on the poor thespians. Well, not always, and anyway as Noël Coward wrote, '*Why* must the show go on?'

But on the show goes whether it's good, bad, or ludicrously awful, and once in a while you get an evening in the theatre that really fascinates. Such an evening occurred in 1976 at the Old Vic.

Farce From My Elbow — The Old Vic

I assumed in my innocence that I was in for an evening of indiscreet wives hiding from cuckolded husbands in a variety of cupboards, and ageing roués turning anticipatory somersaults of desire at the prospect of stolen moments of illicit love. Not so.

The two one-act plays that filled the bill, one French, Feydeau's *The Purging* — and one German, Wedekind's *The Singer,* edged towards quite another frontier, the frontier of Horror. The Feydeau play is about chamber pots. Cupboards of theoretically unbreakable porcelain chamber pots with which the manufacturer is hoping to supply the French Army. By the time Feydeau wrote *The Purging,* in 1904, he was clearly sick of 'Oo la la', and the play comes across as an act of revenge on the audience of the day, whose insatiable thirst for vicarious frivolity had hitherto earned him his living. In *The Purging* you have: one mean, ignorant husband, M. Follovine, one shrewish wife, one awful child, whose constipation motivates the action; one aged pantaloon, M. Chouilloux, one aged pantaloon's wife, one cousin who is suspected of cuckolding the aforementioned pantaloon, and one maid.

Dilys Laye as the wife, relentlessly angry, compulsively cleaning and tidying while personally sluttish, was so compellingly real that she chilled the blood. John Phillips as the pantaloon gave a most impressive comic performance, proud, foolish, a snob, a swank, an idiot — perfect. Leonard Rossiter gave his performance. It was a good performance, a personal and self-made performance, a performance like no other except Mr Rossiter's other performances — save one, which I'll come to in a moment. It was a performance so idiosyncratic that it came out like personalized morse code, and although Mr Rossiter's meaning is always clear, you're hard put to it to make out more than one word in eight. The snarling match between M. and Mme Follovine bleaches what humour there is out of this piece, and I suspect that Feydeau was purging *himself* when he wrote it.

Frank Wedekind's play is altogether jollier. It concerns a pop idol of the 1890s (a Wagner singer) besieged in his Berlin hotel suite by love-sick maidens offering all, a crazy septuagenarian composer with an impossible opera to sell — no, not to sell, for to sell would be to prostitute his art — and a rich woman, the singer's latest amorous discard, who refuses to be discarded. Finally she kills herself gorily, right there on the lino, a piece of ad hoc theatricality which leaves the singer, hardened by years of Wagner, unmoved.

The hotel staff, who are used to such things, treat the incident rather as if a rich guest's dog has misbehaved on the carpet. John Stride handled the part of the irresistible singer with skill, charm and humour. He is a man ruled by contracts, railway timetables, rehearsals and the unglamorous realities of a hard profession. To him sex is as necessary and useful as a good pocket watch, and no more. The obsessions of his admirers he finds faintly boring, a tinge tedious and irrelevant. He points out that if anyone actually listened to the words he sings they'd walk out of the theatre in disgust at such claptrap. He knows that audiences go only to see and be seen, for the excitement of shouting bravo, of sending wine and flowers to their hero, perhaps to kiss him. What he actually *does* is beside the point. He urges on the art-stricken composer, Dhuring (Leonard Rossiter), the ploy of stealing from Wagner as it's only Wagner's music that people want, and suggests that he should become famous as the first requisite to getting his music played, asking him rhetorically to 'Name one famous person who's unknown?' Leonard Rossiter's performance as Dhuring made the phrase a *tour de force* seem somewhat inadequate — hair, teeth, eyes, voice, clothes, gestures combined to paint a most vivid and riveting portrayal. He literally sprayed the singer with a non-stop rant on the subject of the integrity of the artist, ramming home Wedekind's point which is that aspiration and achievement are birds of quite a different feather — as different as nightingale and roast goose.

A. H. and Noises Off

The following represents a typical week of first nights in the London theatre. I reproduce it in full to give the flavour of shows that you may have seen, and, as they opened in 1982, actually remember.

My generation grew up in the shadow of Hitler. He came to power when I was five; when I was twelve I watched his agents systematically trying to knock London to pieces from the air, and when I was seventeen I rejoiced at the news of his death.

You would think that in the thirty-seven years that have passed since then the last drop of conjecture, analysis, and dramatic reconstruction would have been wrung from the sinister buffoon who, had it not been for the even more bloodthirsty and singleminded Stalin, could well have finished up with the whole of Europe under his thumb. As it happens, what passed for right triumphed over what was demonstrably wrong, and the myth of 'the master race' and the thousand-year Reich perished amid the devastation of Berlin in May 1945.

Unfortunately, the Hitler myth didn't perish with it and the unlikely proposition that Hitler is alive and well and living in South America is trotted out yet again in *The Portage To San Cristobal Of AH* at the Mermaid Theatre. A small group of Israeli soldiers prise Hitler, now over ninety and considerably shrunken, from his lair on a mud flat in the Brazilian swamps, and start the long trek back to civilization with their prisoner. They are driven by a sense of outrage, the need for revenge, the feeling that justice must be done and the hope that with Hitler tried and convicted the agony of the Jewish people will at last be quietened. The stuff of epic drama, you'll agree, and if you have never read a book, seen a film or watched a television series that has covered the same ground, the play at the Mermaid will by turns enthral and horrify you.

Unfortunately I have read and viewed so much about the Führer that when Alec McCowen, as Hitler, at last gave voice in a twenty-five minute *tour de force*, I was impressed by the performance but not by what was being said. I don't need to be told that Stalin was a bigger monster than Hitler, that the West turned its collective back on the German Jews in the 1930s and that without Hitler there may not have been a State of Israel. I don't need to be told yet again that the Israelis treat the Palestine Arabs badly, or that the myth of the master-race was only a distorted mirror image of the myth of the chosen people. I knew all these things before I went into the theatre, and two and a half hours of naive rhetoric and stale history, however well acted by however talented a cast, left me numb, not with horror and disgust but with boredom.

Owing to a contretemps with a young lady representing either the Arts Theatre or *Playing The Game,* which is currently being staged there, I haven't seen the play, so I'm afraid I can only quote from the Press handout. '*Playing The Game,*' it says, 'portrays the closed society in a Welsh community which is epitomized by the all-male preserve of rugby. It lays bare the power, political and sexual struggles in the clubhouse, boardroom and bedroom. This is revealed through the men's fear and hatred of women, expressed as impotence, cuckoldry, homosexuality and open violence.'

The Arts Theatre will sell you a ticket for the play at £3 or £4, and there are 'concessions for Rugby Club members, OAP's, and unemployed on production of cards', though why a rugby player would want to go to a play, even at a special rate, to see himself depicted as a violent, impotent, homosexual cuckold, defeats me.

I *did* see *Noises Off* at the Lyric, Hammersmith. Michael Frayn's new farce breaks old ground. It's a tortured romp about a bunch of actors struggling with their problems both on and off the stage and with surprising honesty finding few pat solutions. At least up until the last half dozen speeches in the play there are no pat solutions, but then with the sensation you get when pulling a Wellington boot out of deep treacle, all is well, it transpires, that ends well, and the curtain falls on that comparative rarity, the three-act play. Frankly, the third act is hardly worth blacking up for, as Max Miller is alleged to have told Hutch when they were playing a week at Dewsbury Empire, but there are bigger laughs in *Noises Off* than I have heard in years, and a number of comic performances of high calibre, Michael Aldridge being outstanding. A play about a play is heady stuff for the dramatist, but difficult for an actor, when the real person and impersonated are *both* figments of the imagination, and understandably those in *Noises Off* who play the non-actors — Director, Stage Manager, and Assistant Stage Manager — come out of it better than those actors playing actors playing actors.

Paul Eddington, as the randy, ultimately comforting director, Lloyd Dallas, plays a good hand well, and Yvonne Antrobus as the skinny if thick ASM is delightful. So too is Rowena Roberts playing the ingenue Brooke Ashton playing the ingenue Vicki.

In fact, all do Trojan work, and as I am a fan of Michael Frayn, I will do no more than congratulate him for a great many laughs and tell him that if he cares to leave a sum of money in a certain hollow tree on Hampstead Heath, I will, in return, put him in touch with a gentleman who will tell him what to do with his third act.

The Mousetrap

London is full of tourist attractions and the old-established, long-standing, traditional sights are the ones most sought by visitors to Britain: The Tower of London, Big Ben, Madame Tussaud's, Tower Bridge, and *The Mousetrap*. *The Mousetrap* is, of course, the longest-running play in the history of the theatre: a thriller written by the late Agatha Christie which opened at the Ambassadors Theatre in West Street, WC2 on 25 November 1952.

It transferred to the neighbouring St Martin's Theatre, where it is still running, on 25 March 1974, and it seems there's nothing to stop it running forever. Of course the cast has changed over the years. In fact, one hundred and thirty-two actors and actresses have appeared in it so far. Sir Richard and Lady Attenborough were the first leading players, though in those days they were just plain Richard Attenborough and Sheila Sim. Well, not *plain,* certainly not Sheila Sim.

I first saw the play advertised on its pre-London tour back in October 1952. It was in Liverpool, and I was a young music hall comedian playing at the local variety theatre on the bill supporting Phyllis Dixey. Miss Dixey was a fan dancer who had a great vogue during World War II, starring in a show which ran for years at the Whitehall Theatre. Post-war, she capitalized on her former success with the young servicemen on leave in London with a series of provincial tours. By 1952 her appeal had become largely nostalgic, but there she was, fans and all, up the road from where the new and, as yet, untested *Mousetrap* was bedding down before its London première. Finding myself outside the theatre on the day of the matinée I was undecided whether to see the play or go to the cinema. I tossed a coin, heads for cinema, tails for theatre. The coin came down heads and I went to the pictures.

I never actually got around to seeing *The Mousetrap* until twenty-four years later, at a matinée on 16 October 1976. Certainly half the audience who were there that afternoon could not have been born twenty-four years before and judging from conversations overheard in the foyer during the interval, they had come from all over the world — Scandinavia, the USA, Australia, New Zealand; and, ironically, there was a family party from Liverpool.

But what of the play? Well, it was rather like meeting an elderly and revered politician for the first time. You tend to stare, matching in your mind what you're seeing with what you've heard and read about the celebrity. My first feelings were all to do with the history of the play and not the action — the four million people plus who've actually seen it, the fact that it was fast approaching its ten thousandth performance. The fact that there was still food rationing in Great Britain when it opened, and that our Prime Minister then was Sir Winston Churchill. The fact is that *The Mousetrap* started life as a radio play called *Three Blind Mice* written at the special request of the late Queen Mary for her eightieth birthday. The whole enterprise is a living entry in *The Guinness Book of Records*.

But the play — well, it certainly works all right, the anachronisms being so slight as to be barely noticeable. Odd references to food,

85

music heard on the radio, moments of behaviour (the policeman thinks Ibiza is in Italy) have a period ring to them, but in the main it's a perfectly sound piece of theatre. Obviously, or it wouldn't have run for over twenty-four years. Mind you, the synopsis of scenes tells us that the action takes place in 'The Great Hall of Monkswell Manor — Time: the present', and you wonder whether 'the present' is *today* present or *1952* present. It's well written, of course. Agatha Christie was the mistress of her art and the unfolding of events is far from prophesiable. You are held as the under-currents of emotion surface and ebb — as character after character reveals more of themselves than you first supposed possible.

Agatha Christie was over sixty when she wrote *The Mousetrap*, and I got to wondering how old some of today's leading British playwrights were when it opened in 1852. Harold Pinter (*The Caretaker, The Birthday Party, No Man's Land*) was twenty-two and touring in Ireland as an actor. Alan Ayckbourn (*Norman Conquests, Absurd Person Singular, Absent Friends*) was thirteen and still at school. Tom Stoppard (*Travesties, Jumpers, Rosencrantz And Guildernstern Are Dead, The Real Inspector Hound*) was fifteen and also at school. Alan Bennett (*Forty Years On, Habeas Corpus*) was eighteen and on his way to Oxford. Simon Gray (*Butley, Otherwise Engaged*) was fifteen. Anthony Shaffer (*Sleuth*) was twenty six, and Ben Travers was sixty-six and just getting his second wind. That doesn't prove much except the vitality, the variety and the quality of the London theatre.

The Mousetrap has clocked up a score that is now a legend, unaffected by taste or fashion, and with that in mind what the play is *like* becomes almost irrelevant. It's a play, quite simply, for its audience (many people go again and again) and its audience rustles its programmes, settles back and enjoys itself. Like all institutions from Coca-Cola to Canterbury Cathedral, it's self-propagating. The very fact that it's there is reassuring even if you don't drink coke or go to church.

I feel very attached to the dear old *Mousetrap* in its snug mahogany and red plush theatre with the crimson, gilt-tassled curtain and the orange squash in the interval. I'm almost sorry I've seen it now — it was a pleasure I'd always promised myself and now I've had the pleasure I can't enjoy it again — Oh, I can *go* again perhaps when the cast changes next but there's no time like the first time, and that's come and gone. But at least I know who dunnit. It was... It was... Aaaagh!

Films

The first film I ever saw was either *Green Pastures*, or *The Lives Of A Bengal Lancer*. At a distance of forty years it's difficult to remember every detail, but as far as I can recall the film was about a negro family serving in the British Army on the N.W. Frontier. One son was called McGregor and was a rotter, the other was Mose, a swashbuckling roué who came up to scratch at the right time when the Regiment, owing to a timely intervention by someone called De Lawd, won the Battle of Balaclava. The Colonel of the Regiment was called, as I remember, Catfish.

That's nostalgia for you; Instant Garble.

Because it's what you want it to be, the past is usually all good news, and I would be tampering with my own right to self-deception if I looked back at my cinemagoing with anything but pleasure.

Cinemas were built in the Thirties, as were gin palaces a generation before, as somewhere to go that was better than home, and the Picture Palaces of my youth, the Gaumonts and the Ritzes and later the Odeons and Granadas, were marvels of comfort and excitement. Sitting round a coal fire listening to Harry Hemsley on the wireless was all right in its way, but the cinemas had organs that rose up through the floor bathed in multicoloured lights, and ice-cream girls shining torches on their specialities, and usherettes in uniform, and *two* films — one occasionally in technicolour — and the news and sometimes a Donald Duck cartoon. When the film broke, as it often did, everybody whistled and stamped and then cheered when it got going again. Going to the pictures was an event. Most of all, the cinema was a place you went with your parents — an adult pleasure which you were allowed to share from time to time. Later, when you went alone or with friends you felt on the verge of being grown-up yourself. I was so imbued with the magic of the cinema when I was a lad that it's not surprising (to me at any rate) that for the year or so when I was in the no man's land between school and National Service, I got a job at the Gaumont Palace in Wood Green as a projectionist. I felt like a novice in a religious order about to be initiated into the mysteries of the temple and, of course, my first job was to get the 'tea' for the senior projectionists. The restaurant which was part of the cinema provided meals at specially low prices for the staff, but it was wartime and my only clear memory of what we ate was something described optimistically as Welsh rarebit and which appeared to be an ingenious combination of felt and rubber.

The films we showed were a mixed lot but I remember *Dead of Night* particularly. It was a collection of five short mystery-cum-horror stories by various authors, linked by a most inventive and spinechilling narration involving a man's recurring dream. It starred, among others, Mervyn Johns, Roland Culver, Googie Withers, Michael Redgrave as a berserk ventriloquist, and the marvellous Frederick Valk. It was brilliant, British and, it's almost unnecessary to add, produced at Ealing by Michael Balcon.

In those days the programme ran from Monday to Saturday with three showings a day (with a complete change on Sunday) and the projectors with their carbon arcs and the films themselves with the occasional shaky joints needed constant supervision. Even with your day off you'd have seen the film over a dozen times before it was packed back into its tins (ten reels for a feature) and sent off to its next destination.

When you see them that often the majority of films become tedious, but once in a while there was one of outstanding quality that you were sorry to see go. *The Picture of Dorian Gray*, starring George Sanders and Hurd Hatfield was one such, mainly because the bit where you actually saw the hideous portrait was actually shot in colour in an otherwise black and white film — a piece of theatricality that was amazingly effective. I hadn't read any Oscar Wilde before seeing the film but did so immediately afterwards, and became a devotee. Years later, Marty Feldman and I wrote a parody of Dorian Gray for the radio show 'Round the Horne' — and were able to do it without referring to the book, so powerful were our memories of the original. Come to think of it, Dorian Gray would have made a good story for a

Marty Feldman film, with Marty as Dorian Gray and the portrait in the attic getting handsomer and handsomer.

Another film I remember, but with less affection, from those days was *A Song To Remember*, the story of Chopin's love for George Sanders, sorry, George Sand, and which in spite of starring Merle Oberon set my teeth on edge so much that I cannot listen to Chopin nowadays without breaking into a rash. And talking of Poles, two Polish servicemen, Marek and Rojak, joined our little team in the projection box at Wood Green Gaumont in 1945. They'd had the most extraordinary adventures in the war, being overrun by the Russians in 1939, drifting through Russia in a labour battalion after the Germans invaded in 1940, joining up with the Polish division in the Middle East, fighting with the Eighth Army in the desert and in Italy. They'd been wounded in action at Monte Cassino and were being retrained in civilian occupations before going back to Poland. I had my first lessons in political reality from those two splendid young Poles. Wherever they are now I hope they're thriving.

During the week we were showing *A Song To Remember*, Marek came up to me and said, 'Excuse me, I know the music from this picture but what is the story?' I told him but he didn't believe me. Our chief was a dour man who'd been a projectionist from the days of silent films; from the time, in fact, when projectors were hand cranked. 'Ah,' he'd say, 'in those days you could get home early if you wanted. You just cranked a bit faster.' He'd shown the first talkie in Britain when the sound came from large discs that had to be synchronized with the film. His great ambition was to become the manager of a shoe shop. I know it doesn't sound all that strange an ambition, but it seemed odd to me at the time to want to swap the airy fantasy of Garbo, Dietrich, Hayworth, and Jinx Falconburg for the grim reality of the hammer toe, the bunion and the fallen arch. He used to read books on salesmanship and business efficiency and dream of prize-winning displays of bootlaces and dubbin, and left us younger chaps to see to showing the films, spotlighting the organist and flashing on the advertising slides for Miners Liquid Make-up, Bronx cigarettes, Kolynos toothpaste, and the rest, in the interval between programmes.

From time to time we'd put the reels on in the wrong order (boos and stamping feet), miss the change-over from one reel to the next, and there'd be an embarrassing pause as the second machine was started and the dreaded 10, 9, 8, 7, 6 flashed up on the screen

– and the assistant manager rushed, white faced, into the box and abused everybody in sight while the Poles cursed him back in Lower Silesian and the chief lingered on in the rest room, his head full of Phillips stick-a-soles and blakies.

Sometimes we forgot to rewind the film and showed chunks of it backwards and upside down (boos to crescendo and threats of mass sackings). It was a relief when my call-up papers arrived and I exchanged the silver screen for air force blue. I've never hankered to repeat the experience of projecting movies – but one strange side effect that brief episode in my life has left me with is that having seen *Topper, Mr. Smith Goes To Washington, The Mark Of Zorro, Tales of Manhattan, Heaven Can Wait* and *Step Lively* many many times, I can (when I've had a couple) give an extremely accurate impersonation of the late Eugene Pallette.

How Not To Write A Film Script

The magic of the movies wears off very quickly when you become involved in making them. The whole process is so damnably slow that by the time you get to the end you've forgotten what the beginning was about. Television is the reverse. It's quick — immediate even — and generally forgotten within an hour.

But there was a time when I aspired to being a movie writer. Like the man who got lost in a strange town and, on asking the way to his destination, was told, 'I don't think you can get there from here', I have a feeling I'm not going to be the one who, singlehanded, saves the film industry by writing a smash hit screenplay.

Movies and me have never really got along, mainly because I don't like going out on cold nights to sit up to my ankles in spilt popcorn and plastic soft drink containers while the couple in the row behind indulge in what is euphemistically called heavy petting. Peeking is not my kick, but I bet you I could rewrite the *Karma Sutra* in sound effects if called upon to do so. (Well, there's an offer for you cassette moguls.) It's not that I'm a listening Tom, but it's hard to avoid the adjacent heavy breathing except in really *noisy* films like

Gold or *Earthquake*, during which World War III could pass un-noticed.

As for actually writing films, or indeed appearing in them, my record does not compare with that of Peter Ustinov. To be honest it doesn't even compare with that of Peter the Painter who, if not actually seen, was certainly the star of that celebrated newsreel footage of the siege of Sidney Street.

Where I always seem to fall down is in the mysterious art of selling the screenplay. Now, any fool can write a movie — as the history of the cinema bears witness — and I've written a few myself. I've even written *good* screenplays with Marty Feldman. Actually, Marty and I were kept alive as writers some years back on the strength of a philanthropic film producer having faith in our ability to 'get it right' eventually. Well — it was fun while it lasted. Every year the script would come up for discussion, would get rewritten, money would change hands and then a great silence would fall. The next year it would be the same routine. There'd be a phone call, meetings, a cheque would arrive, the new pages would be delivered and then — silence. It was sad when they finally made the picture. We felt we'd lost an old friend.

Solo, I've never got that far, but I've been propositioned often enough. There are several approaches the writer can expect. The most common is what I call the 'spirit of St Louis' or 'transatlantic solo' approach. This begins with a phone call from an American who says he's a producer and wants to make a film. The dialogue is as predictable as Britain's next balance of payments deficit. It goes along the lines of, 'Say, I heard/saw/read something you wrote. I'd like for us to get together to discuss this very interesting project I'm lining up with Fox/Rank/Universal/EMI/Paramount.' Then comes the meeting — nine times out of ten in an apartment within a hundred yards of the Dorchester Hotel, and generally at around 8.30 am. It's punctuated by transatlantic phone calls. Sometimes there is coffee. Sometimes there isn't. During a lull in the phone calls you are given a much-thumbed copy of a book and asked for an opinion. The book is either called *The Ugliest Girl In Montana, The Day They Screwed Medicine Hat,* or *The Vatican Heist* — well, perhaps not quite, but nearly. I was once offered a scientific treatise called *The Politics Of Population,* and was asked to turn it into a musical. I wish that was a joke but it's absolutely true.

The next thing that happens — to me at any rate — is that you're asked to report back in twenty-four hours giving an assessment of the work and, if possible, a short synopsis. That's where I always go wrong — I *do*. Twenty-four hours later I deliver my brief synopsis, a dozen pages or so, to the flat. No one's home. Hours later I get a phone call from a secretary to say it's been received and that my would-be producer has enjoyed it, is very optimistic but, no, he isn't there. He's had to fly to New York, but she's sure that when he gets back he'll have good news and we'll go ahead.

He never comes back. Maybe he never goes. Maybe he doesn't exist and I've dreamed it all.

The second type of proposition is 'the group approach'. This sort of meeting takes place *after* lunch and you're greeted by the English producer, the American who owns the property ('Barry, I'd like you to meet Hunk Zilch') and an agent. Here the sell is more powerful: 'There is this screenplay see, only we figured you could fix it for X (a well-known actor) who is between pictures and is dying to play it as it is, but they think, you know, maybe it could do with a little fixing...' With this set-up you sometimes get a little money. After all it only needs a little fixing. So you do the fixing — generally a *lot* of fixing — and you all meet regularly for a month or so while the rewrites are being discussed.

This situation has an interesting variation in which the screenplay is said to be flying round the world getting the okay from London, New York and Hollywood. The dialogue is again standard. London and New York love it but Hollywood isn't sure. Couldn't the nurse or the sheriff or the gangleader be American/English/Italian? So that gets fixed and the next meeting produces the information that Hollywood loves it but New York isn't sure. Eventually, of course, it's so mauled that Hollywood, New York and London all hate it. The so-near-and-yet-so-far *schtick* can go right up to the production of the movie. I have sat in an office in Elstree writing scenes due to be shot after lunch and still haven't got them on the screen.

I guess it's me — as I said before, movies and I just don't get on together — and for some years now I haven't even *tried* to write a screenplay. I still have hankerings though. Maybe somebody one day will employ me. After all...look at it this way — I've never had a flop!

I wonder how accurate a guide you get to what a nation is really like by watching its films? Not *very* accurate I suspect, but you do get a fair indication of how people see themselves, or at least how they wish to see themselves and their homeland. For films to be popular they have to project the desired image, something that will lure paying customers into the cinemas and keep them pinned to the stalls for an hour or two. If a film misses that particular trick the folk who made it sit around and blame television.

A martian (and thus, presumably, impartial) looking at the British entertainment industry would see superb theatre, excellent television but virtually no cinema at all. The Grade family, with brother Lew most publicly obvious, and brother Bernard most influential through the EMI company, have had a go at resurrecting the corpse of the British movie; and I wish them luck. (After *March Or Die* and *Voyage Of The Damned* they need it.) Lord Bernstein and friends at Granada wisely now keep out of film making and stick to television, publishing and Bingo. The small, independent producers seem more concerned with making deals than with making pictures. Our supposed Martian would draw the obvious conclusion: there's no call for British movies in Great Britain today.

The French and Italians seem to be going on much as ever, producing a regular crop of good to excellent films concerned with contemporary themes or recent history, and with the French in particular treating real life as a fit subject for drama and humour. The German output is small but gritty, and whatever they're making in Russia, Poland, Czechoslovakia, and Yugoslavia isn't reaching us in any quantity.

But Hollywood — or at any rate Hollywood-type — films still pour out in a never-ending stream. Any cult with a few million dollars can get to make a movie, and sooner or later they turn up at our Odeons, Classics, and ABCs. It is in these films that we obtain a glimpse of the American way of life, and a very strange glimpse it is. We can suppose from what we see that the police are corrupt (*Gauntlet*) and illiterate (*The Choirboys*), the majority of the population are unbalanced (*Rollercoaster, Welcome To L.A., Audrey Rose*), the children are foul-mouthed (*Bad News Bears In Breaking Training*), the adults are worse (*Slap Shot*), and that ignorance, bad temper and intolerance are the norm (*Annie Hall, Audrey Rose, The Choirboys*).

93

This wasn't always the case, as witness *The Glenn Miller Story.* This film was made in 1954 and was even then a period piece, tracing (faintly, I imagine) the life of the trombone-playing bandleader Miller from 1925 to his death in 1944. The title role is played by James Stewart, his wife by June Allyson, and there are guest appearances from Louis Armstrong, Gene Krupa, and Frances Langford. The supporting cast — Henry Morgan, George Tobias, Sig Ruman — are expert. It's well shot, edited and directed (in roughly that order) and the sound recording is as near perfect as you can get. The story is clean, optimistic, humorous and touching. There's not an oath in the entire 116 minutes and it reminds you of those calendars of a pussycat looking out of a boot.

As in all biographies of musicians, every conversation seems to be loaded with significant phrases that'll turn out to be the title of a tune. 'String Of Pearls', 'Pennsylvania 65000', 'Little Brown Jug' are all there — early as symbols, later as fodder for the hit parade. In *The Glenn Miller Story* you begin to suspect that every conversational exchange is going to turn up later as a song title: for instance, 'Stay out of the pawnshops for a while'. 'Want a ride? Get in the back.' 'Good old Colorado "U" ': I could write lyrics for them all.

The motif for *The Glenn Miller Story,* as you probably remember, is the recurring statement that he's looking for a 'New Sound'. The stuff of parody as I, who was a trumpet player in RAF dance bands around 1946–47, remember well. Still, they'll never do the story of 2316554 AC2 Took who never had too much trouble finding new sounds but was hard put to it to find the *right* sound on his recalcitrant instrument.

The Glenn Miller Story starts crisply and is fun while the young trombonist is young and struggling. But it plunges into treacly insipidity when Miller becomes a success, goes into movies, joins the Air Force and allegedly through syncopating brass band music gets the troops to march (almost) in step. After that it's eyes down for the sad ending. It's a nice, warm, gooey film and worth a visit, for there's no doubt that films made for the cinema look better on cinema screens than on television.

What is fascinating is that the American dream in 1954 is totally different from the American dream — well, that's hardly the right word — of today. Then it was home, family and a goal in life. Today it seems that the USA is a land hot of opportunity but disillusion, where the only hope is a retreat into mysticism, drugs or fantasy. *The Glenn Miller Story* was clearly riddled with myths, but the myths were at least affectionate. Today's 'reality' is just plain nasty and I wish someone out there in Beverly Hills would tell us about the good things in the American way of life. There must *be* some.

Red Hearings

It seems odd that the USA, which is arguably the richest and most powerful nation on earth, should from time to time get an attack of the vapours over some imagined threat to its security. Admittedly a country which can boast the biggest in just about everything can equally be supposed to have the biggest idiots. That from time to time these idiots (or crooks, or power-mad bigots come to that) take over is a matter of sad history, but what is strange is that the American people seem to prefer the imbeciles, the villains and megalomaniacs to the well-balanced, the rational and the liberal minded. A case in point was the Hollywood witch-hunts of the 1940s and 1950s when the supposed communist infiltration of tinseltown led to many of the leading writers, actors and producers of the time being blacklisted.

The events of that unhappy period are chronicled in *Hollywood On Trial*. Using a mélange of interviews, film clips and newsreel footage of the House Un-American Activities Committee investigation, the whole grisly story unfolds. The ten men first accused — the accusations consisting mainly of slander, innuendo and hearsay — based their defence on the dubious legality of the committee. They lost. Some went to jail, the group became known as the Hollywood Ten, and the floodgates were open for Nixon and Joseph McCarthy to stage their attacks on the US Congress and the US Army before finally being squashed and discredited. The Hollywood Ten both then and now come across as heroes, their accusers as mean, foolish and despicable. Particularly admirable is the late Dalton Trumbo, a screenwriter of note, who both in appearance and wit resembled S. J. Perelman. His anecdotes of writing for the splendid Otto Preminger are a good in-industry chuckle: Preminger telling him that a scene lacked the genius of the rest of the screenplay, Trumbo replying that if it was *all* good it'd be uninteresting, the poor scene serving to highlight the better ones (a well-known writers' excuse). Preminger's reply was: 'You write it *all* brilliantly, *I'll* direct it unevenly.'

Men like Lester Cole, Ring Lardner Jr., Alvah Bessie, Albert Maltz, Herbert Biberman and Adrian Scott have less happy stories to tell. To lose your job and a hard-earned place in your profession is tough, particularly when your only crime is that of defending the right of free speech. That the trial of The Hollywood Ten was held in public speaks well of American democracy, that it was held at all is an abiding disgrace, and no amount of saying 'it's worse in Russia' changes that.

Me And The Movies

Here, in no particular order of quality, depth or value are my reviews of some of the films I saw in the late 1970s. Most of them, or at least those which are not entirely despicable, have subsequently appeared on television. So, with luck, my comments may have a continuing interest.

Let me own up and say at the outset that I do not regard the film as an Art Form. That is to say I regard it as about as much an art form as a street lamp. It reveals what otherwise would be obscure, and *can* look good while it's doing it. Films can be so pretty or so stimulating or so full of insight that they *become* art but I regard that more as a happy accident, or at best an inspired guess, on the part of the film maker. That's what I think. But then, I'm not a film buff and my ignorance is often monumental when it comes to the fashions and manners of film. I don't regard all Bertolucci's films as good or all Clint Eastwood's films as bad. Of course, I remember those famous and wonderful comic moments in Will Hay's films, but I probably remember them wrong. I accept that Jacques Tati's films can be anything from long to impossibly long but I still regard a Tati film as worth the hours of tedium for the moments of sheer genius.

I have enjoyed films like *Charade, Butch Cassidy And The Sundance Kid, The Sting, Some Like It Hot* and *Blazing Saddles.* I've also enjoyed *Le Jour Se Lève, Orphée, La Grande Illusion,* and *The Discreet Charm of the Bourgeoisie.* I think that some of the Marx Brothers and W. C. Fields films were so badly made that had they not been Marx Brothers or Fields movies they would have been dismissed as trash. Not that I'm saying Groucho, Harpo and Fields were not funny men; but there's more to a motion picture than half a dozen quotable lines. My favourite Fields film is *Million*

Dollar Legs because the story (a small European country is planning to take part in the Olympic Games but woefully lacking in athletes), enhances Field's stance as a shifty wisecracker, since both his shiftiness and his quips have purpose. Archimedes said: 'Give me a lever long enough and a firm place to stand and I will move the earth.' He didn't actually say it to me, so it might have become a little garbled in the two thousand years or so since he said it, but the point is that — however long the lever of humour or tragedy — the firm place to stand in the movie business is the story, and without it the power of the emotions on display is dissipated.

Movies aren't really designed to be seen by a couple of dozen hardened critics at 10.30 am in a preview theatre and so I thought it might be a good idea to go to our local cinema on Saturday afternoon to see *The Spy Who Loved Me*. We were not alone. In fact the cinema was full: audience of all ages, soft drinks being slurped all round, two small boys having a fight in the row in front, adverts, lights up, lights down — the film. *The Spy Who Loved Me* was, of course, the latest in the now seemingly endless line of Bond films except that, to the best of my knowledge, Ian Fleming didn't write a book on which this was based. Frankly, I don't think anybody did. It seemed a computer job; or, perhaps more accurately, an assembly of all the bits that have worked well in previous Bond films.

It contains one mad scientist, one Russian spy (female), one semi-human totally indestructible heavy (a Felix the Cat among screen heavies), one head of MI6, one head of KGB, one man-eating shark, one specially-equipped car (villains for the foiling of), and one happy ending. It's full of stunts and wheezes, chases and fights, chunks of travelogue, special effects, some innocent sex, a modicum of schoolboy smut (well, the schoolboys in the audience shrieked at the various *doubles entendres*) and the indestructible heavy who, after each theoretically terminal discomfiture, emerges brushing the dust off his jacket and looning off into the distance. He'll be back, mark my words.

I know I shouldn't really admit that it was great fun, but it was. Roger Moore is a perky, immaculate 007, always ready with a quip or a kick in the groin as circumstances dictate and in one particularly daft sequence he performs with an air of partially suppressed amusement that is totally disarming. His leading lady, apparently sculpted in margarine, will no doubt make a good living in hairspray advertisements in the years to come. But what can a girl do against so much technology? Act, I suppose, but in such a film you can't have everything, nor, to be honest, is acting much of an asset. The Bond films seem to be becoming more and more like Tom and Jerry and it wouldn't surprise me in the least if the next of these screen epics is produced by Albert Broccoli in association with Hanna/Barbera.

Mixed Bag

Emily is as disturbed as you would expect of someone who has just come out of prison. She drives into a small town, gets a job at a small supermarket on the recommendation of the owner's mother, who is still 'inside', rents a small flyblown apartment and starts (in small ways) to torment a married couple. That's more or less the plot of *Remember My Name*. Who is the mysterious stranger and why does she behave in a way that suggests the film has been licensed by the Commissioners in Lunacy rather than the British Board of Film Censors?

Well, it comes as no surprise that the married man she torments was once married to *her* and that her actions spring from her resentment towards her old husband and his new wife. At the film's conclusion you're a little clearer in your mind as to why she's done it, but I for one was a bit puzzled why Robert Altman and Alan Rudolph had made the film at all. But then I realized that it's a 'woman's picture' — that is to say it's a film about (and for) women who resent their role in life and who feel that a woman's lot (like the policeman's in the song) is not a happy one. What does not help the message on its lugubrious journey is the fact that the woman in this case is clearly as mad as a hatter. Not that I'm suggesting that women are or should be less mad than men. In this as in other matters I'm very much on the side of equality for all.

The film is slow, at times painfully so, but it gets better as more of the plot is revealed and the acting is really very good indeed. Geraldine Chaplin plays Emily, the human poltergeist, with the care and attention to detail you expect from this gifted actress, veering between sweet reason and malevolent violence in a way that is most disturbing. Anthony Perkins as the ex-husband is good too, and Moses Gunn as Pike the negro, whom Emily first uses and then callously rejects, plays with great sensitivity. The best thing about

Remember My Name is undoubtedly the music. The remarkable octogenarian, Alberta Hunter, sings the blues and it's worth making an effort to see the film just to catch those rich mahogany tones.

Weathered teak is how I'd describe Jacques Tati in a *Mon Oncle*. Like all Tati films it meanders along and then suddenly bursts into moments of comic brilliance, only to meander off again. If you've seen it before you'll want to see it again. If you haven't, watch it. Jacques Tati must qualify as the quirkiest film maker on earth, totally committed to his view of the world: the horrors of modernity, the bone-headedness of officials, the intractable nature of artifacts, and the inefficiency of civilization. His own acting style combines in a curious way the neatness of Chaplin and the clumsiness of Stan Laurel. I think he's a genius, a point of view which I happen to know he shares. We once had a long argument in the bar of a Paris film studio between takes for an American Television special I was working on. The nub of the discussion was that while a certain world-famous mime (whom I was defending) merely repeated his polished routines, he, Tati, constantly improvised new comedy. My view was that one was not necessarily better than the other; and while I preferred the latter, the former was also intriguing and stimulating. Jacques Tati, who had somehow got it into his head that I was an accountant, informed me at great length that as I understood nothing but columns of figures I had no right to comment on the art of comedy. He may be right about my lack of comedy. He may be right about my lack of critical acumen, but I still think that at his best Jacques Tati is the world's greatest film comedian.

That Was The Year That Was

Looking back on a whole year's cinemagoing, it's difficult at first to remember any particular one of the two hundred or so movies that fluttered past my reluctant eyeballs in 1978. They're not 'moving' pictures, by the way. Did you know that? Each film is a series of still pictures, each held steady for a fraction of a second in front of the light source by a device known as a Maltese cross. Oh, you *did* know that. Sorry. My own impression of that twelve months is one of continuous blur, and I had to look through back numbers of *Punch* to remind myself whether anything of note was shown. To my amazement I found that the number of good films arriving in British cinemas in 1978 was prodigious, and for what it's worth here are my top ten.

1. *Death On The Nile* — which restored my faith in Peter Ustinov, and was remarkable for the quality of the acting throughout.

2. *Turning Point* — that rare thing, an unsentimental film about the ballet and which was not only well written and well directed but which brought us two talented newcomers, Mikhail Baryshnikov and Leslie Browne.

3. *Outrageous* — a Canadian film with an uncommonly brave story about a schizophrenic girl and her understanding buddy, a homosexual hairdresser, who find strength and comfort in each other's peculiarity. An unexpected bonus was that the film was full of wry humour — for instance 'In Toronto the female impersonators are women.'

4. *Girl Friends* — a soft, nice film about growing up in New York, which brought us the delightful Melanie Mayron.

5. *Heavan Can Wait* — a reworking of the old *Here Comes Mr Jordan,* with Warren Beatty taking most of the credits, but with some excellent dialogue from Elaine May, and a gutsy comic performance from Dyan Cannon.

6. *Stroszek* — Werner Herzog's merciless story of three German misfits who go to the USA and become inevitably American misfits. The most unremittingly honest film of the year.

7. *Pardon Mon Affaire* — jolly French frolic harping on the sexual obsessions of four middle-aged Parisians and in which Jean Rochefort gave an outstanding comedy performance.

8. *Dersu Uzala* — Chinese hunter meets Russian topographer in Siberia in 1902, and they become friends. Full of warmth and insight and a beautiful evocation of man's oneness with nature.

9. *Assault on Precinct 13* — John Carpenter's film about urban violence which, though set in contemporary urban Los Angeles, had strong echoes of the old-style Western.

10. *1900* — the biggest film and, with a running time of four hours, certainly the longest. It tells the story of an estate in the Po Valley from 1900 to the present day, and by doing so

teaches us a lot about Italy in the twentieth century. Bertolucci handled it all with consummate skill, and Burt Lancaster, who I do not blush to confess is my favourite actor, was magnificent.

Having started on a list of favourites it's a temptation to go on and on. I'd like to mention *The Duellists,* which I loved, and *The Shout, Stevie,* and *Oh God.* It was undoubtedly a vintage year, but any penny however shiny has another side and there were some dreadful films too. Among the baddies *The Swarm* would take some beating, the story of killer bees in the USA being of a banality matched only by the woodenness of the acting. But I think there were worse than that. There was, for instance, *Cathy's Curse,* a Canadian horror about diabolic possession, and *The Legacy,* yet again about diabolic possession, and *The Comeback,* which was just diabolical. *The Devil's Advocate,* which surprisingly wasn't about the devil but the attempt to verify or otherwise the saintliness of an army deserter who had made good in an Italian village, wins my prize for the most boring film, and *Viva Knievel,* which starred the maestro of the motor bike, Evel Knievel, was undoubtedly the most cliché ridden. *Herbie Goes To Monte Carlo* would, in most years, win the 'yuck' prize, but escaped the accolade because it was, after all, not designed for adults or indeed, in my judgement, for human beings of any kind. The worst French film was undeniably *L'Hotel de la Plage,* which attempted to cross *Monsieur Hulot's Holiday* with *Pardon Mon Affaire* and failed miserably on both counts. *The Medusa Touch* was the most pretentious failure to be made in England, being even worse than *The Big Sleep,* and *The Wild Geese.*

The prize for the worst film of this or possibly any year must, in my humble opinion, go to *The Stick Up.* It starred, if that is the word, the unlucky David Soul, and I stand by my original thoughts: 'It's played at a sepulchral pace by mismatched actors to a script that would have been rejected by the most banal TV soap opera. It is shot mainly in the dark and has not one single element (apart from a good sound track) that justifies its existence.' It may seem to be unfair to pick on a small-budget film like *The Stick Up,* but if the British film industry is to have any future, people must stop making films as bad as this, or at any rate people must stop releasing them. When paying customers go to the cinema and are disappointed it means that they are less likely to go again.

I may seem to have been abnormally grumpy about the films on

101

offer in my time with *Punch,* but I wrote what I believed then and I must admit, rereading the articles and remembering the films, to feeling as bellicose about the cinema today as I did then.

Here are views, at greater length, on *Close Encounters Of The Third Kind, Assault on Precinct 13, Swept Away,* and *Stroszek.*

Watch This Space

The word around Wardour Street about *Close Encounters Of The Third Kind* was that it was a cross between *Gone With The Wind* and the second coming. Come to think of it, I suppose it does have elements of both. It's certainly long and it's about a strange, unearthly visitation by — well, scarcely a flying saucer, more a flying three-hundred-piece dinner service. An immense piece of special effects, that I suppose at a pinch is worth the two-hour build-up to its appearance.

Before we see it, or indeed those who inhabit this space Leviathan, we've seen funny lights shining on Indiana homes, the electrical equipment in said Indiana homes going berserk, heard a tune repeated by many people none of whom have any connection with each other except, that is, a crowd of some hundreds in India (not Indiana) who rush about humming it in a giant Sing Along With Outer Space. Not only that, but we've seen the materialization of aeroplanes that disappeared into the Bermuda Triangle back in 1945, and other manifestations that — were they to happen to you and me — would have us as an additional burden on the already overstretched Health Service.

Sturdy but sensitive scientists, led by François Truffaut, unravel the mystery of the flashing lights, strange manifestations, etc., and arrange a rendezvous with the extraterrestrial beings in Wyoming. There they play the tune; the space ship answers *fortissimo* on what sounds like a tuba (clearly brass playing is well advanced in the galaxy), and lands. It then disgorges the pilots of the aforementioned aeroplanes lost in the Bermuda Triangle in 1945 plus other humans from other times (we don't get to see them too clearly — they were presumably a sub-plot and that got lost in the editing) and a little boy who's been removed from his Indiana homestead after a good deal of special effects, but who seems quite cheerful about it all when reunited with his mother. There's more, lots more, but I don't want to put you off the film altogether.

Frankly, I thought it was tripe designed and made quite brilliantly for an audience of village idiots. There are good performances from Richard Dreyfus, Teri Garr, Melinda Dillon, and François Truffaut, but the biggest contribution is from Douglas Trumbull who created the visual effects, and they are very special indeed.

One last point: it's not like *Star Wars*. That amiable film appeals to the child in us — *Close Encounters* appeals to our credulity.

It's a far cry from the redneck country of *Close Encounters* to the urban jungle of the poor persons of Los Angeles in *Assault On Precinct 13*. Here in the desert of South LA a police station (the only building on view that doesn't appear to be made of cardboard) comes under attack by a multiracial mob of youths who seek a man who has had the temerity to take his revenge on the callous killer of his daughter. The police station — Precinct 13 — is in the process of closing down, not from lack of custom, one gathers, but in order to move to new premises; and as the attack develops is defended by a mixed handful of cops, lady civilians, and convicts en route to prison. The attack itself is reminiscent of Alfred Hitchcock's *The Birds,* with bullets from silenced revolvers thudding and tearing through the flimsy fabric of both police and station. It's not 'the goodies' who win in the end but a coalition of minorities — a black cop, a white murderer and a middle-class white girl. 'Ho there, symbol-minded Sig', as one of the great Americans once wrote. I wonder, come to think of it, if there are any *great* Americans any more? There just seem to be winners, losers, and survivors. Mind you, I'd put money on *Assault On Precinct 13*'s creator, John Carpenter, to turn out to be a 'great'. His first film, *Dark Star,* shot as and when he could raise the money, was twenty times the intellectual superior of *Star Wars* or *Close Encounters*.

His second, *Precinct 13,* is as good a *Shoot out at OK Corral*-type movie as has been made. An urban Western yet, which he not only wrote and directed but edited (under the name of John T. Chance), and he composed the music too. It's a disturbing film in its implications but satisfyingly complete in its execution.

Swept Away is an Italian-made mixture of *The Admirable Crichton,* and *The Taming Of The Shrew.* Wealthy layabouts on a yacht argue endlessly about the political situation, their hostess, Raffaella (Mariangela Melato), being particularly strident in her contempt for

103

workers generally and the Italian Communist Party in particular. This is more than a little offensive to Gennarino (Giancarlo Giannini), a dockhand whose pop eyes and irritable manner mark him instantly as a hyperthyroid case. Later, a dinghy bearing the unbearable Raffaella and crewed by Gennarino breaks down and eventually washes up on an uninhabited island. (This takes place in the Mediterranean, incidentally, but I for one don't believe you could be on any Mediterranean beach for more than two minutes before being joined by several large, pink German holidaymakers.) They're rescued and we're faced with the fairly unagonizing question: will their relationship last?

The film runs two hours but seems much longer. To be fair, it is very prettily shot, and director/writer Lina Wertmuller obviously knows her stuff. It's a pity that we *also* know her stuff, having seen it all before.

The Dancing Chicken

Life is like the Metropolitan Water Supply — you get out of it what you put into it. The film business is rather like that; a constant recycling of the same old stuff, often looking different but when analysed turning out to be the same familiar ingredients reworked. Just occasionally someone breaks the pattern and turns up with a new form, a few new ideas or a view of the world that is surprising and refreshing, or indeed alarming and frightening. Orson Welles did it in *Citizen Kane,* Fritz Lang did it in *Metropolis. Bad Day At Black Rock,* and *Monty Python And The Holy Grail* in their different ways found a new way of saying things worth saying, and in *Stroszek,* Werner Herzog seems — to me at least — to have made an important contribution to what we know, think and feel about the world we live in. The film blends reality and fiction in a brilliantly subtle way so that you're never sure from one moment to the next what is *real* truth and what is *invented* truth. At a time when most films seem to have little or no truth in them at all it's a refreshing change to come out of the cinema knowing more than when you went in.

Stroszek tells the story of Bruno S. coming out of a Berlin prison after being harangued by the governor on the evils of drink, rather like John Mortimer's story of the derelict wino admonished by the judge, 'You must never drink alcohol again: not even one teeny little sherry before dinner.' On his release Stroszek immediately goes to a bar, befriends a prostitute, Eva (Eva Mattes) who's having pimp trouble and takes her to his apartment where he's greeted by Scheitz (played by Clemens Scheitz) an aged gnome who has been looking after Bruno's mynah bird. After some unpleasantness with the pimps, the trio decide to go to the USA, and Eva whores up enough money to pay for their passage.

They duly arrive in Railroad Flats, Wisconsin, which looks like it sounds, a piece of North American real estate which is barren in thought, word and deed. They put a down payment on a mobile home, which in time is repossessed — Eva leaves for the bright lights of Vancouver(!) — and Bruno and Scheitz take off to rob a bank. It's closed so they rob the next-door barber's shop and with the proceeds Bruno buys a vast frozen oven-ready turkey. Scheitz is captured, Bruno isn't. He flees in a decrepit breakdown van which runs out of everything at a three-dollar-bill Indian reservation tourist trap where the prime attraction is a circus of 'educated animals'. The animals are real, incidentally, their reflexes conditioned to play drums or piano or to dance.

In the end Bruno shoots himself, having switched on all the paraphernalia of the pathetic amusement park and when the police arrive the patrolman calls plaintively to base: 'We can't stop the dancing chicken.' My description must seem like Railroad Flats, but the film is amazing. In an hour and a half Herzog tells you more about Western civilization today than most historians could tell you in a decade, and we don't need Frost and Nixon, Ford and Jimmy Carter to explain the USA. It's all there in the phrase 'We can't stop the dancing chicken.'

Awfully Bloody — Bloody Awful

Coming up to the longest day of the year the films beating a path to your local cinema seem to be vying with each other to be the longest. Or perhaps they only seem the longest. No film distributor in his right mind (and film distributors are notoriously right-minded) is going to screen a would-be blockbuster at the height of the summer, when the pathetic signs reading 'It's cooler inside' are being dragged out of cupboards on the off-chance that the weather will turn hot. Mid-summer, even an English mid-summer, is not a time you would expect to see great movies, so let's see what was on offer.

Well, for a start there was *The Comeback*, and let me say right away I hadn't heard such hearty laughter at a preview for ages. The trouble was that the film is not a comedy. It is, in theory at least, a horror film with a masked madman cutting people up with sickles — a grim reaper indeed — and shots of rats and maggots nibbling away at decaying corpses at strategic intervals. Between these tasteful touches of Grand Guignol there's a limp story of a pop star, Nick Cooper (Jack Jones who really *is* one) making a comeback, and for reasons that would be obscure if they weren't downright silly, is recording his new album in an old, dark house 'forty minutes from London'. The action cuts from this forty-minutes-from-London mansion to the West-End offices of a record company, a Thames-side restaurant, and Nick Cooper's penthouse flat on top of a deserted riverside warehouse. The film cuts so swiftly from one locale to the other in virtually continuous action that I can only suspect that the film's producer, Pete Walker, must know a little-used route to and from central London or have a cavalier attitude to reality. In my experience you can leave the Embankment by car and forty minutes later be not far from the Oval. Of course it's quicker by tube, but with the best will in the world I can't see anyone, however obsessive, taking a maggoty corpse on the District Line even if it is cheaper and quicker.

But this is fruitless speculation when it comes to a film in which nothing makes sense. Mind you, horror films aren't supposed to make sense, they're supposed to make you scream with fright. When the screams are of laughter you suspect that the film makers are a little wide of their mark.

Jack Jones, who these days looks more like the football manager and TV pundit Lawrie McMenemy, than a pop idol, plays his part as well as is humanly possible, is a plausible sex object, albeit with a chest that appears to be covered in Brillo pads, and when you think of what they did to David Soul in *The Stick Up,* must consider himself to be lucky to have been involved in *The Comeback*.

There was no doubt that the best-made film of that summer's crop was Akira Kurosawa's *Dersu Uzala.* It's a shade long (over two hours twenty minutes running time) but it's a thoughtful, tender, warm study of the relationship of two men in a story in which there is no violence, no sex and no bad language. So how do they fill the time, I hear you ask. Well, they do something that would make them the laughing stock of Hollywood and Wardour Street. They use their imagination. Akira Kurosawa and his team paint in delicate colours not only the forests and frozen marshes of Siberia but also the understanding that grows between the Army Captain/topographer and the Chinese hunter who helps him chart the unknown reaches of the Russian outback. Yuri Solomin as Vladimir Arsenyev the explorer is good, Maxin Munzuk as the ageing man of the woods, Dersu, is a total delight.

Dersu Uzala reminds us of the virtues of simplicity.

Strange Doings

The Beast was an attempt to mix art and dirt, and finished up with too much art for the dirty raincoats and too much grunting and groaning for art lovers. It was probably well patronized, and will make a lot of money. After all, *Grease* cleaned up with less to offer; but even greatest fans of Walerian Borowczyk (which when written down looks less like the name of a prominent director than the keyboard layout of a Polish typewriter) will agree that *The Beast* leaves something to be desired. I don't want to appear too dismissive: there are genuinely erotic moments and some good acting. The lighting is fine and the music and editing, if somewhat martial in feeling, are sound and taut.

The story is about a family of loony French aristos who live in a decrepit *château*. There's an old man in a wheelchair, his nephew, the nephew's son — who is a bit strange — and a young woman who spends a good deal of her time getting laid by a black servant. This is not a happy affair, as no sooner do they get into overdrive — as it were — than the poor servant is shouted for and has to dress hurriedly and get downstairs to open a door or pour a glass of port for the visiting priest. This leaves the poor girl staring wistfully at one of the bedknobs (and not only staring at it, I might add). This is no way to keep servants. An English girl arrives with her aunt. She is to marry the son of the house the next day. There is talk of a beast who did something unspeakable to a family ancestor two hundred years previously, and leaden hints such as, 'He manifests himself every two hundred years.'

The English girl has erotic daydreams in which a rose figures prominently (an entirely new view of Interflora) and a nightmare in which the beast has its way with her in the woods. The end could be described succinctly as Exit Rogered By A Bear, and such is the emphasis on the erect male member that the film could usefully be subtitled Bedknobs And Broomsticks. The whole thing is laughable, and I suspect much of the mischief is intentional. I hope so. For it to be unintentional would make *The Beast* a very bad film indeed.

Not Angels But Choirboys

The Choirboys is about a group of Los Angeles policemen who can barely muster a decent emotion between the lot of them. They're painted by director Robert Aldrich as lecherous, stupid, depraved, perverted, shifty, incoherent, bestial thugs. How faithful the film is to the book on which it is based I do not know as I haven't read it, but I hope that the author is as upset as I am by the film. Aldrich paints a picture of such unredeemed squalor and brutality that I'm almost tempted to wish for the return of some kind of censorship, if only on the grounds of taste. I'm not so naive as to suppose that all policemen are angels, and at a pinch I can believe that the Los Angeles police are worse than most, but surely they're not the ugly bunch depicted in *The Choirboys*. If the film is a reasonably accurate representation of the truth, then the USA is in a frightening state of disintegration. If it's untrue then how can people be allowed to take such liberties with the facts? Is there no law?... Oh.

Mad About Ludwig

In a week's viewing dominated largely by utter rubbish it was a relief to have seen at least one film that seemed to have been worth the trouble of making. It was described as 'Visconti's lost masterpiece', though where it was lost and who found it isn't clear to me. It is in fact his 1972 epic, *Ludwig*. Apparently Visconti cut the original version from an uncomfortable three hours plus to the present two hours fifteen minutes. At that it still lies a mite heavy on the senses but as Visconti makes every frame of his films count, the effect is (almost) entirely ravishing.

Ludwig tells of the poor mad King of Bavaria from coronation to watery grave, leaving out much but implying plenty. He was Wagner's patron at a time when all Munich was against the composer both for his music and for his mistress, Cosima von Bülow, whose husband, though with them throughout, affected not to notice the liaison. Eventually even Ludwig had to bow to the storm of public disapproval and get rid of the unsavoury trio (played in the film with just the right mixture of bravura, slyness and sycophancy by Trevor Howard, Silvana Mangano, and Mark Burns) and turned his unstable yearning for the artistic into a spate of castle building. His marriage is skirted (*did* he marry Sophie?), the growing eccentricity and homosexuality are touched on, his teeth rot, his throne is taken from him and he finished up eluding doctors and guards and drowns in the lake.

The film ends with the thought, 'Did he fall or was he pushed?' but it is irrelevant to Visconti's story. Helmut Berger as Ludwig looks suitably haunted throughout from initial introversion to the final watchful, controlled lunacy of the by now totally mad monarch: a performance of delicacy and shadows. Romy Schneider as Elizabeth of Austria, Ludwig's only real confidante, is alive, dominant, and wholly admirable. Miss Schneider is so compelling that when she's on the screen the pace seems faster, the sets brighter and, that rare thing in a Visconti picture, humour seems only a whisper away. If for nothing else see *Ludwig* for Romy Schneider giving one of the major performances of her career.

Who Swallowed The Formula?

Somebody Killed Her Husband is a confection which the publicity handout informed me was 'a love story leavened with laughter and spiced with suspense in the tradition of the zestful sophisticated mystery-comedy of the late 30's and 40's, reminiscent of The Thin Man films but contemporary in mood and style.' Well, if the men who made the film choose to tell me that, who am I to argue? But if they believe it in any way, shape or form (except in the most general sense, that Jeff Bridges is a man and Farrah Fawcett Majors is a woman) they are in dire need of medical help.

Jeff Bridges (son of Lloyd and brother of Beau) plays Jerry

Green, an assistant in the toy department of Macy's department store. Enter Farrah Fawcett Majors as Jenny More, with a stroller – that is to say, a pushchair — and a recalcitrant infant. Jerry falls for her, they lunch in the park, exchange some leaden philosophical remarks on the subject of sharing food, and fall in love. Her husband is a business-obsessed insurance man (not the bicycle clips and fawn raincoat type, I should add, but the high rise duplex apartment decorated in a manner the Shah of Persia wouldn't turn his nose up at type of insurance man). Anyway, Bridges and Fawcett Majors are upstairs: they hear hubby's voice with A.N. Other downstairs, go down and tell him the gladsome news that they're in love and find him (the husband) with a knife in his back.

All this happens in about ten minutes of screen time, possibly the world record for love at first sight to corpse in the kitchen, and inevitably — why are you yawning? — decide a) they can't go to the police, b) they will solve the murder themselves, and c) there's more to this than meets the eye. There's *not* a lot more, incidentally, and as the bodies pile up at an alarming rate and the cast isn't that big to start with, they (and you) soon realize who the murderer is. Jeff Bridges is a very good light comedy actor and acts his head off throughout. Miss Fawcett Majors looks as if she's being operated by remote control, wears a series of high-fashion casual outfits, shows emotion by emitting high-pitched squeaks, and appears to have more than her fair share of teeth. The toddler is fine — a Baby Leroy in the making if ever I saw one. The credits carry the puzzling title 'Farrah Fawcett Majors' make-up designed by Way Bandy'. Whoever it was who designed Miss Fawcett Majors ain't saying.

Post-scripts

I packed in film reviewing for *Punch* in February 1979 and vowed never to do it again. However, to help out a friend I did a three-week holiday stint in May/June 1981, deputizing for Margaret Hinxman on the *Daily Mail*.

I found a shift in emphasis from films about the occult and diabolic possession — my three weeks in the dark presented me with three murderers whose evil deeds vied with each other for gory horror.

The First Deadly Sin

The opening title sequence creates an atmosphere of menace and puzzlement. Figures lurk in doorways. Ice-picks thud into the skulls of pedestrian New Yorkers. On an operating table a scalpel makes a bloody incision. Down a dark street a murderer lopes away, his grisly business completed for the night. What is it all about you ask. Is this the one about the homicidal surgeon? But as the credits end having announced variously the participation of Jack Priestley, Joe Napolitano and Fred Caruso, we see the gnarled form of our old friend, Francis Albert Sinatra, in the person of Edward Delaney, a detective sergeant in the 17th precinct, on the verge of retirement and on his last case, an 'orrible murder. Not having had the advantage of seeing the aforementioned opening sequence, he doesn't know that the murder weapon is an ice-pick (well, an ice *hammer* actually) and as nobody else on the force seems remotely interested in this outbreak of mass murder — one presumes it's commonplace in the Big Apple — the good sergeant plods off to solve the murders using the traditional police methods of elimination, civilian assistance and luck.

He doesn't really need the extra aggravation of a spate of ice-pick murders as his wife Barbara (Faye Dunaway) is in hospital having had a kidney removed, and is sinking slowly. Faye Dunaway doesn't have much to do but look ill, which she manages with her habitual skill, and Sinatra, his face looking as if it'd been slept in, has most of the action: interrogating, deducing and bribing his way to the final confrontation with the rich, young, white Anglo-Saxon psycopath.

The Fan

The following week the psycopath wandering the streets of New York was the deranged fan of Lauren Bacall. Not, of course, that he's the only fan of Lauren Bacall (I'm one too), nor is this the cause of his derangement, but the film explores what happens when hero worship reaches extremes and lands the worshipper, not to mention the one who is worshipped, in the soup, or tomato sauce, or whatever it is they use to simulate blood in the movies these days.

The Fan is gory almost to a fault and one wonders why the producers found it necessary to make such a blood-stained film in the first place. But of this more later. Let me describe the plot, which is as slender as the elegant Miss Bacall herself. Young Douglas Breen (Michael Biehn) is a long-time admirer of Sally Ross (Lauren Bacall), a stage and movie star. Frustrated by only ever receiving replies to his fan letters from the secretary, Belle Goldman (Maureen Stapleton), his emotions boil over and he attacks the unfortunate Belle with a razor in the subway, which — as is common in this type of film — is deserted at the time. Later he attacks a young man, who is rehearsing with Sally Ross for a new musical, in the swimming pool of the YMCA. The pool is *not* deserted but the psycho makes his escape and next strikes the star's maid, and a homosexual pick-up whom he then incinerates.

As a climax he does in lovable old Pop, the stage door-keeper,

Hilda, the star's dresser, and finally corners the object of his bizarre attentions in the deserted theatre after the successful first night of her show.

Until recently one would have thought the ease with which a homicidal maniac can elude the police, passersby and even James Garner, who plays Lauren Bacall's semi-estranged ex-husband, far fetched. Today, however, with the Yorkshire Ripper, John Lennon's murder and close shaves for Pope and President alike still very much in our minds, it's all too real. A maniac looning round New York armed with a cut-throat razor seems small beer by comparison. What, then, is the point of a film like *The Fan?*

Well, there's a brief speech from Miss Bacall towards the end of the picture in which she turns on her assailant and gives him a mouthful along the lines of 'decent people are sick of psychos, muggers, terrorists and the like and we won't stand for it any more'. I'm not quoting directly from the film but that's the gist of it. The producers don't offer much in the way of a solution to the problem except the concept of retaliation, which is, when you think about it, a pretty miserable argument. The other ingredients of *The Fan* are fairly run of the mill. Would-be witticisms, semi-sophistication, mediocre music and some fine photography, direction, and editing, wasted — to my mind at least — on a hunk of dross. I say dross because, and I ask rhetorically, to whom will this film appeal? The bloodthirsty, the ghoulish, and the deranged possibly, but what kind of film company seeks such people as its cash customers?

But maybe it's me who's out of step.

When the lights went up in the cinema after the chilling dénouement, I fell to imagining (as a comic relief I must admit) a film in which a deranged barber haunts New York with an electric razor with which he shaves people; removing the sideburns, moustaches and other hirsute appendages of the people who made *The Fan.*

Nighthawks

It's night in New York City. Down a dark, wet street, past the now familiar piles of garbage, a lonely woman is walking. In a doorway lurks a sinister figure. A street lamp gleams on a flick-knife. 'Good grief,' you're saying, 'not another one about the grisly doings of New York muggers? Not another innocent pedestrian foully slain? Not the same old New York of *The First Deadly Sin,* and *The Fan?* Not that same old garbage?' And, mercifully, the answer is *no.* It's

113

not the same, as the 'lonely woman' turns out to be Sylvester Stallone in drag, part of a crack New York Police Street Crime Unit. The other part is Billy Dee Williams, and as respectively Deke Da Silva and Matthew Fox, they make a very efficient pair of crime fighters — more commendable even than Superman I and II, as they manage much the same feats but without what I suppose one must call, with apologies to Granada Television, the Krypton Factor. I'd have happily watched Stallone and Williams cleaning up the city for ninety minutes or so, but the story, as it were, pulls out to reveal wider issues.

Wulfger, a terrorist (Rutger Hauer) is abroad; literally, as we see him in London laying waste to a big department store, and then in Paris where it seems he's getting the thumbs down from various terrorist organizations as he's a bit too bloodthirsty even for them. Also Interpol are on to him and so after a little cosmetic surgery and a shave, he heads for New York to re-establish himself as the world's number one hit-man.

He has an even more ruthless sidekick in the shapely person of Shakka (Persis Khambatta) who, it is said, kills without a trace of emotion, a sort of homicidal Buster Keaton, but they have to contend with Inspector Hartman of Interpol (Nigel Davenport), who forms an anti-terrorist squad from the New York Police Department Crime Unit and this, of course, means that Da Silva and Fox are back centre screen.

To be briefer than the film deserves (for *Nighthawks* is tense, gripping and, although bloody, thrilling) let me just say that events pile one upon another, and we arrive at last at a thoroughly nail-biting climax.

For a would-be spine chiller to really chill the spine, the man who is doing the chilling has to be both real and frightening. This, Rutger Hauer as Wulfger achieves perfectly. You really feel that here is an ice-cold clinical killer.

As the cop who learns at last that to catch a terrorist you must think and act like one, Sylvester Stallone brings all that we've come to expect from his previous performances, and which have made him, in my book, one of that rare breed, a genuine *star*. Billy Dee Williams, Nigel Davenport, and Joe Spinell, fast making himself indispensable to this type of story, are all excellent, and in *Nighthawks* we are given a film that was worth the trouble of making and, provided your system can stand the shocks, one that is certainly worth the trouble of seeing.

Post-post-script

The British Film Industry, if there can be said to be such a thing, seems permanently in a state of crisis. Mind you, when you see some of the films that are made in this country a crisis seems unsurprising.

There are honourable exceptions, of course, to the makers of garbage masquerading as British films, and Bryan Forbes is one such exception. I admire him but my admiration stops short of adoration. Thus when I came to report a National Film Theatre Interview with the versatile Forbes I placed my tongue firmly in my cheek and wrote my piece in the form of a letter from a Cockney movie buff.

THE ENCHANTED COTTAGE,
WOOD GREEN, N22

Wednesday 19th June 1978

Dear Bryan,
Me and my mate, Mike,* went along to the NFT a couple of weeks ago to hear you telling us about your career in the movies. Well, Bryan, I must say you seem to have seen it all and done the lot, acting and directing and producing and writing and being an executive and everything. What with one thing and another you can't have had a moment to yourself.

Whistle Down The Wind is my favourite of yours. I thought it was smashing, and that bit they showed at the NFT where the vicar was going on about vandals stealing the lead from the church roof for poor Hayley Mills, who only wanted to know if her kitten would go to heaven, was dead good. Ditto *The Angry Silence* with your mate, Richard Attenborough (now *Sir* Richard, of course. Any chance of a tickle in that direction for you?) Your Hollywood film, *King Rat,* was a good one and all. Likewise many others. And I see we've got *International Velvet* to look forward to in the near future. You told us at the NFT that it might be Nanette Newman's best film yet, and said how she came to you and said, 'Tatum O'Neal is a natural,' which is very generous from another actor and must have knocked you all of a heap. I mean to say, film stars are not noted for their generosity, usually being on a big ego trip and

*Michael ffolkes, the cartoonist and chronicler of movies for *Punch*.

115

tend to be a bit out of touch with reality. Come to think of it, you have Nanette Newman in a lot of your films. I suppose that her being your wife it could be embarrassing if you used some other actress, and besides the extra income probably comes in handy when, as you said, you often don't know where your next job is coming from. My mate, Mike, thinks she's smashing, and I say good luck to you.

It was interesting at the NFT when that lady in the audience said you weren't very good at comedy — and you sort of bristled and said, 'What about *Only Two Can Play*?' Hear hear. And, of course, *The Wrong Box* where Peter Sellers used a kitten as a blotter.

Still you can afford to smile when you're criticized, because you don't have many flops, do you? And I admire the way all through your career you've been able to step into the breach at a moment's notice — like you were telling us about how in *Cockleshell Heroes* you were re-shooting the same scenes that the proper director José Ferrer had just done. I didn't quite get the point of that. Was he a rotten director? Then there was *Whistle Down The Wind* where you stepped in for Guy Green, and *The L-Shaped Room* where you obliged when Jack Clayton dropped out, and *The Mad Woman Of Chaillot* which John Huston was supposed to have done. Hence the expression 'well, that's show business', I suppose.

You mentioned film critics once or twice in your lecture at the NFT and it sticks out a mile you don't like *them* very much. What was the phrase you used about your friend's film *East Of Elephant Rock*? Oh yes, you said 'the critics urinated on it'. Well, Bryan, I suppose they've got their job to do. After all they're not employed to go round saying that *everything's* good, and I might add that I saw *East Of Elephant Rock* myself and think that whatever the critics did on it was well deserved. Of course you're quite right to say that television has killed the cinema and, as you pointed out, TV can get good writers. Now why's that do you think?

All in all it was a good evening. It's not every day you get a chance to hear the personal views of one of our leading film makers. Come to think of it, you're about the only leading film maker we've got.

Yours truly,
Aubrey Greenspan

Part three

Reflections

Oh, to be in England!

One wet Thursday I received a letter from Bryn Frank, the Editor of the magazine *In Britain,* saying — in part — 'our aim is tourist promotion and any slant you can give in this direction would be most desirable'.

Well, since then I've taken a slanted look at about most aspects of life in the UK from cooking to street markets. My wife and I have been sent in a Rolls Royce to cover South East England. (It was assumed at the Brighton hotel at which we stayed that we were having 'a dirty weekend'. I had to pay in advance, I was overcharged, and when the drinks I ordered up to our room arrived the waiter winked slyly and said, 'Haven't I seen your face before?' By now thoroughly irritated I answered, 'Very likely. I'm a magistrate' — and he shot out of the door like a startled rabbit.) I've been sent to Hereford and Worcester, Yorkshire, and to *The Mousetrap.* I've also been to the Highland Games at Braemar, and the Three-Day Event at Badminton. When they couldn't think of anywhere else to send me, I was asked to comment on the seasons. It goes without saying that when you write for a travel magazine all geese are swans and all clouds have silver linings — so if the note of healthy optimism in the following pages gets you down... write something rude in the margin.

'Summer time and de living is easy' goes the song. 'Those Autumn leaves drift by my window' goes another ditty — and 'Walking in a Winter Wonderland' trills a third. But I suppose, this being the season for suppositions, that spring comes out top of the seasonal hit parade with endless numbers about rabbits and chickens and Easter eggs and April showers and Mendelssohn's 'Spring Song' and Christian Sinding's 'Rustle Of Spring' — 'More sinned against than Sinding', I remember once hearing a BBC announcer describe that ever (indeed over) popular melody. Percy Scholes, in the *Oxford Companion To Music,* calls 'Rustle Of Spring' 'ubiquitously popular' and who am I to argue. Much poetry has been written about the spring, many rhymes and conceits, frivolities and fancies as heady as the season itself. From the vulgar adaptation of Alfred, Lord Tennyson's verse —

> *In the Spring a young man's fancy*
> *lightly turns —*
> *To what the girls have been thinking*
> *about all winter.*

to the frivolous words of Edna St Vincent Millay —

> *April comes in like an idiot,*
> *babbling and strewing flowers.*

which I find charming, apt, and possessing a gaiety that belies the words. Not for Miss Millay the stolid gloom of Thomas Carlyle who wrote of 'long stormy springtime, wet contentious April' or T. S. Eliot, not at his jolliest in *The Wasteland* admittedly, who penned these lines in that epic poem —

> *April is the cruellest month, breeding*
> *Lilacs out of the dead land, mixing*
> *Memory and desire, stirring*
> *Dull roots with spring rain.*

Well, T. S. Eliot can have his gloomy forebodings. Give me the inestimable Will Shakespeare with his

> *...spring time, the only pretty ring time,*
> *When birds do sing, hey ding a ding, ding:*
> *Sweet lovers love the spring.*

120

which may not be as you like it, but suits me as it must have done Will all those springs ago.

I cannot leave the poetry of spring without quoting what is probably the best known, and possibly the most often misquoted, verse in the *Golden Treasury*. Robert Browning's 'Home Thoughts From Abroad'. The one that begins 'Oh, to be in England, now that April's there.' Oh, you would-be Robert Brownings who aren't in England, let me whet your appetite, brush up your nostalgia, kindle a spark of desire that will be fanned in the months to come into a positive blaze of lust to be in England, or indeed Wales, Scotland, or Ireland in April. Let's have more of the Browning poem:

> *Oh, to be in England,*
> *Now that April's there,*
> *And whoever wakes in England*
> *Sees, some morning, unaware,*
> *That the lowest boughs and the brushwood sheaf*
> *Round the elm-tree bole are in tiny leaf*
> *While the chaffinch sings on the orchard bough*
> *In England — now!*

A pause to digest that and we'll move on.

The beauty of living in a country where the seasons are so vividly marked is that you can feel Nature's clock ticking away inside you and begin very quickly to adjust to the rhythm that shows you each day something ever so slightly different. I live in London, near Regent's Park, and there in the green centre of the urban mass the stroller can mark the passing of the days by the size of ducklings on the lake, or by the catkins hanging on the willow boughs. The elms, alas, are gone. As 'die back' affects the blue gums of Australia so the Dutch disease has polished off the great and stately elms. But what remains is not a desert. Oak, ash and chestnut; sycamore, poplar, and plane trees, fir, holly, lime and spruce stand tall in copse and garden. The mulberry flourishes in England still, and I could take you to a private garden in Sussex in which a former owner has planted every tree and shrub mentioned in the Bible. A devout man, both horticulturalist and scholar, he spent many years collecting, planting and nurturing this unique array, not for his own pleasure but for those who would come after him. In Sussex, too, there is Hever, once home of Ann Bullen, better known as the unhappy second bride of Henry VIII, Anne Boleyn. Hever, unlike the 'biblical' garden is open to the public, and in spring it's at its best, as are many gardens of stately homes and palaces — the grass not yet tramped brown by the visiting throngs.

In April the chestnuts too are at their best. I'll digress, if I may, about the chestnut, prince of trees (the oak is king) and to me the absolute symbol of the English spring. There are, of course, two types of chestnut — the sweet chestnut with its tempting and much prized fruit (or nuts to you) which whether roasted, pulped for stuffing, or served glacé is delicious; and the horse chestnut. The horse chestnut is so called, so Gerard in his *Herball* of 1597 tells us, 'For that the people of the East countries do with the fruit thereof cure their horses of the cough.' In the West, nowadays at least, horse chestnuts — that is to say the nuts themselves — are hardened, and attached to a length of string delight the young in head in the game of conkers.

But did you know that there is Chestnut Sunday? It is celebrated in the London area around Ascension Day, because the Chestnut Avenue at Hampton Court usually bursts into bloom at round that time. I understand that Paris has some small reputation for its chestnuts in blossom — why not visit both places and compare them? Come to think of it, what a wonderful thing to say to people when they ask you where you are vacationing: 'We're going to Europe to compare the chestnuts' — a sure-fire conversation-stopper if I ever heard one.

But we have strayed from our Browning and stopping only to consider the chaffinch and the fact that the male of the species is gaudy in his red waistcoat whilst the female is discreetly garbed, as if by Yves St Laurent, in pale grey and lemon, we move to the next stanza of the poem. Browning writes:

> *And after April, when May follows,*
> *And the whitethroat builds, and all the swallows!*
> *Hark, where my blossomed pear-tree in the hedge,*
> *Leans to the field and scatters on the clover,*
> *Blossoms and dewdrops — at the bent spray's edge —*
> *That's the wise thrush; he sings each song twice over,*
> *Lest you should think he never could recapture*
> *The first fine careless rapture!*

If you ask me, Robert Browning is going over the top a bit there. The thrush is either wise, or he's up to his beak in careless rapture, offering, presumably, the avian equivalent of diamonds and mink to his intended mate. Now is this the action of a wise bird? I ask you — but you see I am captivated too by Browning's heady verse — and I think now of spring and a particular tree in a particular spot in Regent's Park, near Queen Mary's Rose Garden where on any day in spring you can see thrushes, both song and mistle, chaffinches, blue tits, coal tits, great tits, sparrows, robins, magpies, jays, and starlings. Well *I* have seen them all there in spring — and that's in the well-manicured heart of one of the world's most delightful public gardens. Browning, writing from memory, remembers the country-side:

> And though the fields look rough with hoary dew,
> All will be gay when noontide wakes anew
> The buttercups, the little children's dower —
> Far brighter than this gaudy melon-flower —

Ah, a hint of melancholy among the exotica and more than a whiff of nostalgia. When I crunch through the snowy winter or the crisp and brittle dead leaves of autumn, or stroll idly in the long June days, I too am nostalgic for the English spring, knowing only that one day it will return and that I will be able to say with a full heart: 'Oh, to be in England now that April's there'.

Excuse Me, Which One Is The Queen?

Badminton is a great place to be if you're a horse. You're petted, fawned on, brushed, stroked, patted, you get to meet Royalty — if you're very lucky you even get to be *ridden* by Royalty. It's not a one-way traffic. In return for the attention and loving care you receive you have to walk sideways and backwards with extreme precision, jump over enormous obstacles and generally act in the highly-trained and competitive manner usually only expected of football players.

'The Three Day Event is an equestrian version of the modern Pentathlon... which demands almost every activity of which the horse is capable' — so says the Badminton Horse Trials programme. Almost every activity which can be mentioned in polite society, I need hardly add, and if nothing else, Badminton is the epitome of politeness. The Three Day Event, which being British actually takes four days, is held at the ancestral seat of His Grace the Duke Of Beaufort, about one hundred miles from London in the direction of Bristol. It's in a sort of English Bermuda Triangle of countryside which might be Wiltshire, Somerset or Gloucestershire, but which anyway nowadays seems to be called Avon. I suppose that means that the Young Lady of Gloucester made famous in limerick has now become the Avon lady.

But does Badminton the place have any connection with Badminton the game, I hear you cry. Well, the answer is, yes. My research informs me that Badminton the game originated in the North Hall of Badminton House and that it was invented by the six daughters of the Duke of Beaufort. It is believed that the rules were drawn up by the National Badminton Association in about 1850. And in 1950 the Association played some games in the North Hall to celebrate the centenary.

But what of the Three Day Event and the horses? The trials consist of three disciplines — Dressage, Cross Country, and Show Jumping. Points are deducted for errors and the one, or rather pair (horse and rider), who have most points at the end of the Event are the winners and receive the Whitbread Trophy. Whitbread and Co. also add a not inconsiderable amount of cash (about £20,000 in real money) to be split among the owners of the top twelve horses. A number of points can be lost at Dressage, which I'm told is fascinating if you're a keen horse person. My knowledge of horses comes almost solely from a brief acquaintance with a milkman's horse in the 1930s, a briefer shot at learning to ride a maniacal pony in 1940, and watching racing on television since then.

To see the great beasts hop, step and skip round in circles, their riders motionless on their backs, is a puzzle I never really unravelled, even with the help of a 76-page booklet issued by the British Horse Society and designed to tell you all you need to know about Dressage. To the layman the book seems a treatise on 'How to become a contortionist'. It tells you such things as 'Item 403 *The Walk* . . . a horse should not be asked to walk on the bit at the early stages of his training.'

Item 404 on *The Trot* contains the information that 'The forefeet should touch the ground on the spot towards which they are pointing.' It adds, 'All trot work is executed sitting unless otherwise indicated.' Item 411, describing the movement called *Shoulder-in,*

124

says 'The horse is slightly bent round the inside leg of the rider.'

The BHS handbook informs you that errors to watch for in Dressage are grinding of teeth and tail swishing (this only applies to the horse), the use of the whip (riders only), and carrying a whip more than one metre long excluding the lash — (I assume this applies to riders as well). Bandages or boots, except equi-boots — whatever they might be — or any sort of blinkers are forbidden. Many kinds of bit (that's the bit that goes in the horse's mouth) are allowed, and they all have extraordinary names, my favourite being the 'Egg-butt snaffle without cheeks', which to my mind sounds more like a sobriety test than a piece of equestrian equipment, but then Dressage is not for the ignorant bystander, in other words me.

The big day of Badminton is undoubtedly the Saturday, the day of the sixteen-mile Cross Country. This is the bit that most people come to see (more than a hundred thousand most years) and it's fast, dangerous and tricky. The competitors leap, or at least attempt to leap, thirty-four obstacles spaced round several miles of Badminton grounds, which include hedges, fences, ditches, fallen trees, sunken roads, or any combination, and there is a jump over a (simulated) jetty into a (real) lake and a leap out of the lake over a boathouse. This jump attracts the biggest crowd on the assumption that the riders are likely to fall in — an expectation which is amply fulfilled. Just to look at the massive obstacles makes you feel a touch faint, and the thought of leaping them astride a horse built on the lines of Mount Olympus tends to bring on the vapours or have you reaching for a handy hip flask. The jumps are named with a mixture of prosaic earthiness and country archness. Nothing could sound more ordinary then the Woodpile or Park Wall, but there's all of Surtees (the Charles Dickens of fox hunting) in Vicar's Choice, Huntsman's Grave and Lamb Creep. With an eye to the principal sponsor of the event, there are Whitbread Drays and The Whitbread Bar.

But as with any country event anywhere, the jumping is only a part of the occasion, and at Badminton a tented village springs up in the fields adjoining the main arena where you can buy anything from a 50p plate of seafood to an £8,000 equestrian ornament, or a diamond necklace. Now why should anyone go to Badminton and buy a very expensive piece of jewellery? I don't know, but they do. Other goods on display in myriad tent-shops include saddles, anoraks, toffee, hamburgers, white wine, coffee, hats, paintings (example, a hound £185, and what might have been a cow £150, guaranteed done in oils with frame included).

At Badminton you can buy fur coats, Wellington boots, crêpes suzettes, popcorn, Guinness, milk, cider, shooting sticks, riding habits, Landrovers, German sausages, oysters and deerstalker hats. There's a police station, a crêche, ambulances galore, pubs, clubs, and comfort stations. The GPO is there, and the fire brigade too. There's even a private airfield nearby. The atmosphere is as English as Cheddar cheese and the Bath bun, and you can be forgiven for thinking that the twentieth century is happening somewhere else. The occasion attracts town and country alike and visitors from abroad abound, but wherever people are from they seem to have reached common agreement on what to wear. Men tend towards cavalry twill trousers, check caps, anoraks and Wellington boots. The women wear anoraks and Wellingtons, tweed skirts and sensible stockings. On their heads they wear either knitted hats or headscarves. Fashion note: the Wellingtons are a particular brand in a kind of slime green, and obviously the 'in' thing. A lot of younger women wear men's cloth caps too, but whether this is an idea borrowed from the fashion magazines or whether the rag trade picked up the idea in the stable yard, I've no way of knowing.

Many visitors carry shooting sticks which, as everyone knows, is a stick for sitting on and not for shooting with, and is a sound investment for Badminton. The Show Jumping and Dressage take place in a well-seated arena but the Cross Country is — well, cross country, and while waiting for the next rider to come a purler at the Keeper's Rails or the Faggot Pile, it's a shooting stick or nothing if you wish to rest awhile.

There's little more I can say about the Badminton Three Day Event except to assure you of its excellence as both spectacle and occasion. Looking at my notebook — some time after the event — I find my remarks are, to say the least, random.

Item Princess Anne entered the arena for the Dressage in a shower of hail — the only one of the day. (Hail must be a particularly Royal phenomenon. When Her Majesty the Queen arrived at the Highland Games at Braemar there was a similar shower.)

Item Dogs everywhere — the sort of dogs that aren't called just plain dogs but are either terriers or hounds. They are on leads — usually the charge of the children of the family (and Badminton is, above everything, a family occasion) the rule seeming to be that the smallest child leads the largest dog. Dogs seem to come in pairs,

126

threes or more. One lady I spotted had six Pekinese in tow.

Item Colonel Weldon, the principal architect and guiding light of the Badminton event, told the assembled Press that he hoped a man would win. 'I think we should have chaps riding for England.' In fact, the year I was there the first three places went to women — Jane Holderness-Roddam, Lucinda Prior-Palmer, and Jane Starkey (who only lost by a hyphen). These young ladies seen from close to are surprisingly small, particularly in relation to the horses they ride, their complexions a tribute to the open-air life. (Or perhaps the Avon Lady had paid them a visit.)

Overheard Young lady rider to horse who's just stumbled over a particularly nasty jump — 'You were bloody lucky to get away with that.' An onlooker, as the Royal party stands chatting to the Duke of Beaufort and officials — 'Excuse me, which one is the Queen?' Another bystander to friend, subject: the weather — 'Once you get out of the wind it's almost bearable.'

The weather *is* variable in this part of England in April, which is a polite way of saying a polar bear would have found it a bit on the cold side, so if you're planning a visit, wrap up. You can always shed a sweater or two if and when the sun comes out.

My last memory of the Three Day Event was of Badminton House (built in 1682) glowing in the rays of the early evening sun, with the Royal Standard fluttering at the masthead, and the private aeroplanes of the wealthy zooming off to heaven knows where. The rest of us earthbound mortals scraped the mud off our Wellington boots, got into our cars, revved up the motors and headed for home.

Summer is I-cumen in

Summer time, for me, is the stuff of memories: memories such as June, July and August 1940 when a strange calm seemed to hang over the country and elderly gents tied carving knives to broom handles ready to face Hitler's panzers, should they come, while the countryside sprouted brick and concrete pillboxes — still there today, defiant as the Martello towers built against the possible arrival of another tyrant who never made it to Britain, Napoleon Bonaparte.

Pre-war summer for me, as a child, meant swimming every day in our local municipal pool until August when, for two giddy weeks, we'd go to Dorset or Devon — Father, Mother, brother, me, in a small black, forever going-wrong motor car of a make long submerged in a welter of multinational cross-breeding. Today cars are rarely black and rarely break down, but delightfully Devon and Dorset are still the same. That, I suppose, in a world that seems to change by the hour, is the West Country's greatest charm. Sailing, fishing, bathing and honey still for tea, and strawberry jam, and rich, thick Devonshire cream and scones, and brown bread and butter, and mystery trips.

In my youth no seaside resort, even the one so lacking in amenities that it was known in our family as 'the last resort', seemed capable of facing the summer visitor without the line of coaches promising varieties of mystery tour, the price depending on the length of the trip and whether or not a Devonshire tea was included. Today, recently converted to non-smoking, I find Devonshire teas a temptation to be resisted as although neither I nor my loved ones are that worried about my expanding waistline, it does seem foolish to give up one bad habit (smoking) for another, over-eating.

Still, I dare say that faced with a true Devonshire tea, good intentions would disappear like morning mist around Exeter Cathedral. The simple truth is that after a lifetime, well, an adult lifetime at least of being a heavy smoker, I'd forgotten that I had ever had taste buds and the sensual pleasures of eating are just hitting me. Not just today's lunch or yesterday's dinner either. I keep being reminded of food long ago, when I was a boy. Kippers for breakfast, scallops and bacon for supper — and on Saturdays, cockles, and winkles (known to my ancient East Anglian grandmother as 'wrinkles') and shrimps, and prawns and whelks. Does everyone on earth like seafood, particularly the small crustacea, as much as the Londoner? Parts of London are built on a foundation of oyster shells, and jellied eels are an East London speciality fit to rival the northern English delicacy, tripe.

'Tripe', my daughter — proudly airing new knowledge when she was eight, or thereabouts — assured my wife and me 'is a fresh-water fish.' There spoke a London child to whom mussels were almost the first solid food she'd tasted but who had never even *seen* tripe. My wife and I assumed she'd confused the white crinkly stuff, which makes both Yorkshire and Lancashire hearts rejoice, with the trout... which is a different kettle of fish entirely. Some people don't regard Britain as being a gastronomic paradise, but some people could be wrong. Let me list a few of the wonders, and — if you have a map of the British Isles handy — imagine the variety of countryside as well as the rich diversity of food that this brief list conjures up. Lancashire hotpot, Yorkshire pudding, Banbury tarts, Eccles cakes, Wensleydale cheese, Stilton, Suffolk Punch (no, sorry, that's a breed of horse), Arbroath smokies, Aberdeen Angus beef, Welsh rarebit, Irish stew, Cornish pasties, Bath buns, Bath chaps, and Bath Olivers. The last three all originate from that delightful grey stone eighteenth-century haven of elegance and good living, the city of Bath. The city where the Romans bathed, the contemporaries of Beau Nash *drank* the water, and from whence, in the early days of radio, a BBC announcer was heard to say, 'We now take you over for a recital of chamber music from the Bath room at Pump.'

129

I spent a happy week in Bath back in my acting days during the annual Bath Festival, when other attractions included an Evening With Ruth Draper, the celebrated *diseuse,* and John Barbirolli, the conductor of the Hallé Orchestra. Neither of these fine artists is still alive, but the Bath Festival still flourishes every year in late May and early June.

In Britain in summer festivals abound; one of the most curious, literally unique, is the celebration every fourth year (leap year) of the trial for the Dunmow Flitch.

This ritual goes back into the dark ages, or to put it another way, nobody remembers who started it, but the event now consists of a trial (or trials) for those seeking to prove their marriage is a perfect union. The Dunmow Flitch, a side of bacon, is the prize. The trials are held in a huge marquee in a handy field in the Essex village of Dunmow — the occasion outgrew the village hall many years ago — and the event is staged in front of a large and good-natured crowd who cheer their favourites and attempt, by their applause, to sway the jury. The whole enterprise is mounted as a proper trial with judge, jury ('twelve youths and maidens of the district'), prosecuting and defence lawyers, rules of evidence, and stiff cross-questioning. The jury are persuaded for or against the claimants, as the would-be perfect couple are known, by the wit and skill of the honorary QC's, generally show business celebrities co-opted for the occasion, and it's not unknown for the proceedings to end in general hilarity. If the jury finds for the claimants they receive the flitch, and are then ceremoniously chaired round the town. The losers get a smaller piece of bacon — and everyone concerned has a good time. Make a note in your diary for next leap year, Dunmow, Essex. Near Stansted Airport. If you can make it, as I did in 1982, I'm sure you'll finish the day, as I did, impressed and amused by the truly loving couples who put their private lives on the line for the sake of tradition, entertainment, and a side of bacon. (Mind you, I could be prejudiced — I acted as counsel for the defence, and like a bewigged Perry Mason won both my cases.)

Summer and hilarity go together — the crowded beaches of the larger seaside resorts, the song-singing country pubs, the cosmopolitan crowds thronging the London theatres. In Britain summer is a time to let your hair down and, forgetting the real world for a week or two (or more), indulge in your favourite fantasy. Fantasy is what theatres are about and although nowadays much of our fantasy comes via television or radio (along with all too much

130

reality) the theatre as the arena of heightened emotion can't be beaten.

London not only has many excellent theatres but is full of good restaurants too (good heavens, not food again!) and thus after an evening spent in a handsome theatre watching fine acting and then a supper of some sumptuosity (try Sheekeys in St Martin's Court, off St Martin's Lane, or The Grange in King Street, Covent Garden) you'll appreciate what a delightful place London in summer *can* be.

Of course, almost everything that I've mentioned can be enjoyed, or at least experienced, at other times of the year, and I know of no one in the 'Come to Britain' movement who does not like to stress the pleasures of the 'off season', but it's my sort of summer I've been writing about, and it's my hope that one day you will experience some of the pleasures that have made me say, along with James Russell Lowell —

What is so rare as a day in June?
Then if ever come perfect days.

After all, summer is what *you* make it, and I am amazed to realize that I have managed to get through a piece about the British summer without even a mention of Ascot, Lords, Wimbledon, Glyndebourne, Henley, the Proms, Glorious Goodwood, the British Amateur Golf Championship, Trooping the Colour, the Robert Burns Festival, the International Eisteddfod, or even the event held at St John's in the Isle of Man on the fifth of July, Tynwald Day. To be honest, I don't know what the last one is, but one of these days I'm going to make it my business to be in the Isle of Man on the fifth of July just to find out. For the moment I'm engulfed in another waft of memory and am thinking about myself when young, walking along a sandy beach with a shrimping net, on my way back to the boarding house and one of those amazing Devonshire teas.

Son Of The Beach

I have a theory that the reason the French Foreign Legion is such a popular subject for movies is that the action takes place on a beach. Admittedly you don't think of the Sahara Desert right off as a beach, but if you exercise your imagination a bit it's not difficult to see that it *is* one, and the fact that it stretches from the shores of the Mediterranean to Timbuktu merely adds the dimension of size to what at Bournemouth and the Cap d'Antibes is the bit that divides the land from the water, the bit you lie on to get brown — the bit that children build castles out of, lose their spades, beachballs, buckets, swimming trunks in, and on which — according to the advertisements of my youth — bronzed bullies kicked sand in the faces of seven-stone weaklings.

So, Beau Geste, the Red Shadow, Rudolph Valentino, and the rest went to the Sahara not simply to join the Legion or to ravish maidens or to rally the tribes of North Africa — they, their creators, and we willing conspirators were reliving childhood fantasies of spending our entire lives on a beach. No more homework, school dinners, Wellington boots, cod liver oil and snuffly colds. In our minds at least we were bronzed desert hawks, do-or-die, devil-may-care rascals.

Sandy beaches are potent symbols. Why else do so many of us go back to the seaside every year? Why do resorts with no sand import it in shiploads for the greater delight of visitors? Why, when lake, forest and mountain bring spiritual comfort and ease do the travel brochures and our own expectations of a good vacation rely so heavily on sand? Of course the popularity of resorts doesn't rest entirely on sand. If that were true, Nice and Monte Carlo would still be sleepy fishing villages — but there's no doubt that sand, apart from insinuating itself into every crevice of the body and stopping your wrist watch, offers a powerful stimulus to the imagination.

When I was working in Hollywood in the late 1960s, my best discovery was that if you drove far enough along Sunset Boulevard you'd come to the sea — the Pacific Ocean to be precise. Once there a left turn would take you to Santa Monica, turn right and you'd be in Malibu, or better still Zuma, which boasts an enormous beach. There my daughter, who was not quite two years old, would paddle happily in the freezing ocean and my wife and I would speculate on why we were the only people in sight. Mind you it was December/January but after the rigours of an English winter it seemed positively balmy. Anyway, the sea air made a change from smog, and being on a beach made certain that there was no chance, even by accident, of seeing American television — a bonus even if the temperature had been fifteen degrees below.

I have seen Bondi Beach in Sydney, but in winter and deserted. Most of *my* beach memories are of Europe and summer

132

holidays. In Italy, having to pay for the privilege of sitting in a row of deckchairs at right angles to the sea, staring at an identical row of chairs occupied by jolly Dutchmen turning pink as one watched. Walking along a beach west of Bordeaux and finding myself suddenly, to my acute embarrassment, in the midst of a nudist camp. (At Cannes there's nude bathing too, but usually only during the film festival.) Of strolling at night with my wife along the seashore at Biarritz and suddenly being dazzled with light and finding we were unwittingly a part of the Son et Lumière. Then there was the occasion at Antibes when there was a sudden commotion on the beach — a crowd gathered, ambulances and police arrived — much shouting and then great laughter. What had happened was that an elderly, excitable Frenchman had seen a young man carry a supine, bikini-clad girl from the sea, lay her gently on the sand and administer the kiss of life. With a cry of *'au secours'* the elderly gent had rushed to the life-guard who had in turn alerted the local emergency services. A crowd quickly gathered round the young man offering help and advice in many tongues. It took some time for the man to explain (he was Norwegian) that he was on his honeymoon and the young lady was his wife, and that after a refreshing swim he was expressing his ardour. His wife, far from drowning, was merely limp with bliss. When all this finally got through to the crowd there was laughter and a round of good-natured applause. All the world loves a lover, but the French love lovers best. Allegedly erotic films such as *Goodbye Emanuelle, Madam Claude,* and the like, frequently include scenes of lovemaking on the seashore (I suppose the most famous was the scene between Burt Lancaster and Deborah Kerr in *From Here To Eternity*).

Maybe it's my age, maybe it's just my Englishness, but I cannot think it possible to be amorous half in, half out of the water. No sea is *that* warm, and rolling around in damp sand doesn't seem conducive to highly charged sexuality. I won't even go into the possibilities of the whole business being accompanied by a sort of Greek chorus of shrimps, sardines, crabs and squids.

The thing that has caused me most emotional upheaval at the seaside is losing children. I have four, and at one time or another I've lost most of them. They were all found again subsequently, I need hardly add, but I think that most parents will agree there's nothing quite like the horror of looking up from your deckchair to find your child has vanished into a beach full of strangers. My older

133

daughter vanished on the beach at Viareggio when she was four. I found her half an hour later being consoled with ice cream by a chambermaid from the hotel who was enjoying a day off on the beach and had recognized her. My older son vanished though not, now I come to think of it, on a beach, but in a hotel in Paris. He was found in due course, fast asleep in bed in another bedroom two floors down. The room was occupied by a single lady, but as she was out and he was six I put the incident down to somnambulence rather than precocity. My younger son, when aged five, went missing at La Baule in Brittany ('the biggest beach in Europe') and was gone for hours. We were frantic, but he was returned to the hotel by the local police after a piece of detective work that would have been a credit to Hercule Poirot. Needless to say, ten minutes after the incident he was as right as rain and scoffed about half a pound of caviare, having been placated with canapés by the hotel proprietor and acquired a taste for the stuff.

My youngest, mercifully, has a sense of direction, but we keep an eagle eye on her just the same. With luck she'll be eighteen before she gets lost on the beach, but by then I suspect she'll be *furious* if I go looking for her.

Cannes Do

A welcome early summer jaunt, for those hardy souls whose job it is to watch movies, is to Cannes. I went for the first time in 1978. Sore feet, acid stomach, eye strain, a nervous rash and a desire to enter a monastery. That's what going to the Cannes Film Festival will get you if you're not careful. Also if you're not careful you can pick up the tab for a lunch for four that comes (roughly translated from the French) to £194. It didn't happen to me, but the look on the face of my host when *l'addition* came his way will haunt me for years.

On the other hand, where but at the Cannes Film Festival could you get to meet Miss Nude America promoting a film of that name disappointingly dressed in a one-piece bathing suit, but who promised to strip if the *mistral* stopped blowing? Where else could you see a PR man dressed like a refugee from the 8th Army the better to promote his clients, or go to the cinema at 8.30 am and have your ticket taken by a man in a dinner jacket?

Where but in Cannes during the festival could you sip champagne at a reception given to honour a star so popular that he arrived with eight bodyguards and no one could get near enough to talk to him? Or stand in a group chatting and realize that of the five people you're with four of them are world famous film producers?

Where else but in Cannes does the trade press, *Screen International, Variety,* and *The Hollywood Reporter* arrive daily and free? Of the three, incidentally, I found *Screen International* the best, mostly because it described *Punch* as a 'prestigious magazine', and because its editor, Peter Noble, injects a rare dry humour into his daily gossip column. He certainly gets about, that Noble. You leave one party saying goodbye to him, go to another and find him already there, glass in hand, greeting you like a long-lost brother.

For the English contingent, Peter Noble is a sort of unofficial master of the revels, knowing who everybody is, knowing everything that's going on, introducing people to each other — producers to backers, directors to starlets, husbands to wives…

I must confess that having expected the beach to be covered in nude starlets I was disappointed. What the beach was mainly covered in was the sea (there was a high wind, grey sky and large waves most days) — or members of the local bomb squad detonating an explosive device discovered earlier in a projection booth at the Palais de Festivals. Whether it had been placed there by a frantic publicist, a madman or a critic was not discovered — and come to think of it, how could anyone have told the difference?

The festival is, of course, for buying and selling movies and setting up business deals and announcing forthcoming production plans ('A $120 million splash from Lord Lew') but there's an awful lot of films to see, not to mention a lot of awful films to see. On one typical day you could have watched, if there were enough of you, one hundred and twelve films including the Swedish *Men Can't Be Raped,* an American SF film, *The Clones, Lemon Popsicle* from Israel, *Pas A Pas* from the Lebanon, *Fearless Fuzz* from Italy, and from Japan, *Message From Space.*

There are so many films that you tend to lose the desire to see any of them, particularly as the cinemas and viewing rooms are invariably crowded with earnest Scandinavians, and you have to have the appropriate pass, or a glib line of patter in Lapp, to get in.

The crowds at Cannes are prodigious and people rush in great droves from screening to reception, and from press conference to screening like disorientated lemmings. The cinema may be dying in Britain but it's alive and well worldwide, and Cannes is its Mecca. Stars still guarantee crowds, and promoters and producers seem to get caught up in the general euphoria, signing up everybody in sight, frequently each other.

The toothy Farrah Fawcett Majors, who I must confess I had hitherto last seen on a poster on the wall of John Travolta's bedroom in *Saturday Night Fever,* made an appearance at the festival and was duly put under contract by John Daly *and* Lew Grade, and indeed from what I can gather is about to be in every film made in the next three years. Miss Fawcett Majors said she was flattered by the attention and said, 'As I do more roles I will become a better actress.' We can only hope so.

No such shyness inhibited Muhammad Ali, who confessed to those present at his press conference to promote *Freedom Road* that he was sure that he'd go down in history as one of the world's greatest actors, a title to add to his self-awarded accolade as 'the world's most popular human'.

Apart from 'the market' what is Cannes about? Well, it gives film makers a chance to explain their films to the world's press. Louis Malle defending his picture *Pretty Baby,* which is about child prostitution in New Orleans in 1917, said *á propos* censorship, 'When people don't approve of my work because of its subject matter I tell them that I don't approve of murder but there's a hell of a lot of films on that subject around.' I couldn't get the views of the thirteen-year-old Brooke Shields who plays the child hooker in the film as she wasn't at the press conference. As one wag remarked, 'It's past her bed time.' The Cannes Film Festival seemed dominated by the orgasm and the films were just as sexy. In *An Unmarried Woman,* Alan Bates makes love to Jill Clayburgh. In *The Shout* he makes love to Susannah York. In *Coming Home* oral sex is featured, Jane Fonda being at the receiving end of John Voight's attentions. In *The Chant Of Jimmy Blacksmith,* a long and well-made Australian film about the struggles of a part-aboriginal to find acceptance in white society in the 1890s, it's a good old-fashioned skirts-up/trousers-down affair in the barn. In the Spanish entry, *Los Restos Del Naufragio* sex happens off screen, but in *Bye Bye Monkey,* the official Italian entry and as weird a piece of film making as we'll be seeing for some time, you lose count of the number and variety of sexual encounters, the most memorable being, I

136

suppose, Gerard Depardieu being gang-banged by a group of actresses from an off-Broadway theatre group. If the film ever comes to Britain I'll write about it in length, but to be truthful I'd need to see it a second time to have any clue as to what it's about.

My last memories of my first Cannes are as incongruous as the festival itself... of chatting to Otto Preminger before a reception and his wistfully extolling the delights of the White Elephant restaurant in Curzon Street... of the stretch of the Croisette where suddenly the language stopped being polyglot with American overtones and became exclusively Italian — a scene from *The Godfather* without subtitles, as the Cinecittà contingent hawked their wares to each other... of a friend of mine surveying two hundred diners in evening dress at a free binge and saying, 'Look at them — they're all *mad*. They could have done this on the phone.'

Those Autumn Leaves

To write about autumn without quoting Keats' 'Season of mists and mellow fruitfulness', leaves me writing, as it were, with one hand tied behind my back; 'Autumn nodding o'er the yellow plain, comes jovial on' as James Thomson, also writing about the season, in the eighteenth century so aptly said, is no substitute for Keats and his 'Close bosom-friend of the maturing sun'. All right, if Keats is out who is in? Longfellow, perhaps, with his description of Autumn, which —

> Comes like a warrior
> With the stain of blood upon his brazen mail
> His crimson scarf is rent
> His scarlet banner drips with gore
> His step is like a flail upon a threshing floor.

Well, that's all a bit violent for me. I'm much more into mellow fruitfulness, particularly in the matter of port wine which after a long hot summer one can, in the cooler evenings, drink at one's ease when one is sitting beside what Robert Louis Stevenson described, although possibly not in this context, as 'autumn fires'. But whether you go for Robert Browning's view of Autumn and its 'Mute appeal to sympathy for its decay' or consider the season to be Edwin Way Teale's time of 'scattering abroad' or even agree with Thomas Wolfe in his belief that 'all things point home in old October', the real problem is to know when autumn actually is.

I mean, when does it stop being summer? When does Autumn, in the great relay race of the seasons, hand over the baton, as it were, to Winter? Let's settle for the start date being the first of September, the anniversary of the day when Henry VI of England ascended the throne at the age of nine months (in 1422) and when Louis XIV of France, the 'Sun King', departed this life in 1715 after a reign of nearly seventy-three years. And let me suggest that the last day of autumn is the fifth of November, still celebrated in England with fireworks as a tribute to the unlucky conspirators of the Gunpowder Plot who, in 1605, failed to do what many of us have wanted to do since — blow up Parliament.

However, as that is neither a mellow thought nor particularly fruitful, let us look at what is in store for us in the autumn. If you're a sportsman, or rather sports watcher, there are many events to choose from including the European Golf Championships held at Sunningdale, the Royal Highland Gathering at Braemar in the beautiful Grampians, which if you have a drop of Scots blood in your veins or an eye for colour or a liking for the bagpipes played en masse and at length, is not to be missed. The Meeting is invariably attended by members of the Royal Family and their friends, and some years back while I was covering the event, one of the *royal* friends happened to be a friend of mine too. We were both attached to the BBC at that time, and seeing my friend the week after the Games I mentioned I'd seen her with the Royal Party. Her response was 'Why didn't you come over and say "hello"?' Other annual events of a sporting kind in September include International Sheepdog Trials at Blair Atholl, also in Scotland, the St Leger at Doncaster, and the Waterloo Bowling Handicap at Blackpool (of interest to any member of the numerous bowling clubs in Sydney who might be looking for an excuse to visit the UK in the Autumn). Then there's greyhound racing at Wembley in London, a cricket final at Lords, and in one of the most beautiful settings in England, the grounds of Burghley House in Lincolnshire, the Burghley Horse Trials.

October brings a nice mix of motoring events and arts festivals; more horse trials, this time at Chatsworth in Derbyshire, the home of the Duke and Duchess of Devonshire; and the Nottingham Goose Fair, and Autumn 1982, finished on a high note (if it happened to be your interest) with the thirty-ninth International Ploughing Championships in Northern Ireland on the third and fourth of November.

Of all the many, and there are *many*, events held every autumn, the one I most hope to get to is the Northern Antique Dealers Fair in Harrogate. It's not that I'm a great collector and neither am I enamoured of antique dealers, but I *do* like Yorkshire. It is a part of England I first visited more than thirty years ago (in autumn) when I was a young comedian taking the first faltering steps along the road to, well, let's say a career in showbusiness.

Anyway, in 1951 I'd won a radio talent contest and on the strength of that was appearing for a week at the Empire Theatre, Leeds. I stayed at theatrical 'digs', which had the traditional attributes of a permanent smell of cabbage in the hall, noisy plumbing, lumpy beds, no visitors after ten at night and no ladies in the rooms. I subsequently stayed at better boarding houses, and on recent trips have resided at either the elegant Queen's Hotel or the modern Dragonara. In 1951 the former establishment was beyond my means and the latter not yet built. In those days food was still rationed and the economic revival seemed a long way off. Churchill had just returned to power after six years in the wilderness and the industrial towns of Yorkshire were still much as J.B. Priestley had described them in the 1920s and 30s. That is to say they were sooty and cobbled but vibrated with life. Then, as now, there were two Yorkshires: the 'posh bits', the tearooms with their musical trios doing the best they could with Lehàr and Strauss, and the elegant stores, but there were also great bustling markets and tripe shops, and fish and chip shops, and pie shops and brass bands, and smoke-filled music halls, and life and laughter, and still, in some isolated areas, gaslight. It was probably ghastly but I loved it and revelled in my visits to the county of the white rose. Huddersfield, Halifax, Bradford, Barnsley, Wakefield, Sheffield, Rotherham...

On a recent visit with wife and daughter (now fourteen) by car, I was both amazed by the changes, and cheered to find traces of the old places. Holmfirth, for instance, hasn't changed and is much the same as it was when Bamforths, the postcard people, tried to start a British film industry back before the First World War. The weather got them in the end. Mists, with or without mellow fruitfulness, are not the ideal weather conditions in which to make movies. The Dales are the same as they were and from the Pennines to the sea and from Sheffield in the south to Ripon in the north there's so much country and so much variety it fair takes your breath away. But touring isn't all rushing about in cars, however good the motorways are, and we found, my wife, daughter and I, some splendid hotels and restaurants — the Box Tree at Ilkley, the Old Swan in Harrogate, the Royal Station Hotel in York (and also the Chandelier restaurant), and possibly best of all, the Wentbridge House Hotel at Wentbridge. However, Yorkshire isn't places any more than autumn is the time when the football season begins. It's people, and Yorkshire people have a sort of guarded exuberance that makes them a joy to meet and a delight to know.

At the Wentbridge House Hotel we met and chatted to a family of three, mother, father and son. They came from Barnsley a few miles away, and were regular visitors dropping in for lunch or dinner or for the weekend as the fancy took them. It was my daughter's first experience of Yorkshire and though we number several Yorkshire people among our friends she hadn't come in contact with Yorkshire people on their home ground. The good-natured banter and the broad vowels of the father (put on for her benefit) captivated my daughter. The mother and I talked 'weather', no uncommon thing among the British — the port flowed — it was a warming and enlightening evening.

I've noticed before that wherever in the world you go there, at the other end of your travels, is a Yorkshireman ready to tell you about the local beer or the state of the government. It wouldn't surprise me to arrive at the Pearly Gates to find St Peter with a broad Barnsley accent recommending the local draft nectar, in just the way that I arrived for the first time in Wagga Wagga to be greeted by a 'tyke', as they affectionately call themselves, who informed me graphically of the state of the local pubs. Not that I'm suggesting that Wagga Wagga is at all what I imagine Heaven to be like . . . but I'm sure you take my point. The true Yorkshireman is genial and ubiquitous.

When I think of Yorkshire I think of autumn and this quotation from Hal Borland's *Sundial Of The Seasons*: 'October is the fallen leaf but it is also a wider horizon more clearly seen. It is the distant hills once more in sight and the enduring constellations above them once again.'

And do you know what's so splendid about autumn? We get one every year.

The Braemar Gathering

A sign carved in granite told us 'You are entering the Highlands', and although the scenery from Aberdeen to Aboyne is fairly spectacular, the road from Balmoral to the scene of the Gathering at Braemar is downright beautiful. One look and I christened it 'calendar country' on the grounds that it would be impossible to take a photograph that wouldn't grace a 'Wonders of Britain' calendar. Heather purple against green, pine trees as straight and stiff as guardsmen, lush meadow grass reaching up the flanks of Highland cattle munching vacuously as if waiting for Landseer to come along and paint them, lochs lead shot with silver as the light caught the ripples. Stark hills, grey above the tree line green below, crenellated castles like moulds for some expensive Victorian dessert, flags fluttering from flagpoles, neat, dark tarmacadamed roads — high overhead a wheeling eagle — I felt almost drowned in sensation. It was almost too good to be true and I half expected the whole thing to be hoisted up like some theatrical backdrop to reveal a brick wall and a sign that said 'No Smoking'. But it was real enough. Surprising to me only because it was my first visit.

It's not surprising that the Royal Family stay at Balmoral whenever they can. Queen Victoria acquired the property in 1852 and Albert the Good had the existing house rebuilt as a castle in the Scottish baronial style. It was completed in 1855 and Queen Victoria described Balmoral as 'this dear paradise', a point of view that I wouldn't quibble with. The River Dee wends its broad, unhurried way through this part of Scotland over a bed of granite boulders, winding picturesquely between hills, through valleys, under hump-backed bridges until it empties itself into the kipper-infested North Sea at Aberdeen.

We arrived at Braemar early on the morning of the third of September, the we in question being not the royal 'we' but me and the far from royal Mike Wells, a photographer, who from my experience of riding as passenger in our hired car is a frustrated motor-racing driver. There's a definite streak of Juan Fangio in Wells, but in deference to my grey hairs he kept to rational speeds, rarely going over 60 mph down narrow, hairpinned single track roads, and keeping to a sedate 70 on the main highways. So a combination of zeal and Wells' driving got us to the scene of Braemar Royal Highland Society Gathering approximately an hour before anyone else. There were a few officials there, of course, stern kilted Highlanders with shepherd's crooks and the faraway look of men who know where a glass of malt can be found if the need arises.

Braemar is a 'dry' gathering and, as there's nowhere in a kilt to secrete a hip flask, stays dry and thus good-natured all day. If you wanted alcohol you could go to one of the local hotels in the village, but if you didn't there was a vast refreshment tent where cheery Scots ladies dispensed tea, coffee, soft drinks, hot dogs, buns, sandwiches and chocolate biscuits throughout the day. As the crowd at the Gathering numbered, at its peak — that's to say when the royal party arrived — somewhere between thirty and forty thousand souls the ladies in the tea tent were kept busy. If it wasn't for the huge crowd Braemar would be like any other well run village fête, but the staggering number of foreign visitors adds a cosmopolitan air to what would otherwise be just a local sports day. If you *are* from abroad there's the Overseas Visitors Tent where in exchange for a signature in the visitors book you get a sprig of lucky white heather (I wonder if anyone has thought of marketing 'unlucky' white heather for masochists) and thus sprigged can pin a slip of paper with your name and address on to a map of your home country. When I first visited the tent at about 9.30 am the map of Europe boasted one solitary name — a Miss Triemann from somewhere not unadjacent to Liechtenstein. New Zealand boasted two 'flags' and Australia three. By noon there was a crop of Belgian, Dutch and Luxembourg name tags, the seaboards of the United States and Canada were all but obscured and the map of Australia was dotted with name tags from N. Queensland to Tasmania. Every state was represented except the Northern Territory. Where were you Alice Springs? We missed you.

If you had come to Braemar you could have met Elena de Blacio of Caseria in Italy, Irena Madelova from Czechoslovakia, G. Bakkeli of Harstad in Norway, and Antony Mananyi from Ghana to name but a few of the folk who had come to this tiny speck on the map from as far afield as Japan, Iran, Israel, Costa Rica and India.

What had they come to see? Well, there was the piobairreached open (that's a solo bagpiping contest), putting the sixteen-pound ball (there was a contestant from Kerrimuir who was presumably throwing the Ball of Kerrimuir), there was sword dancing, hammer throwing, tossing the caber, relay races, tug of war, and an event described in the programme as 'throwing the fifty-six pound weight over Bar, one hand', an essay in strength, concentration, skill and pointlessness that defies description. There were many other events, fifty-four in all, and the whole was lubricated by pipe music from a number of pipe and drum bands who for the delight of the Royals and the assembled *hoi polloi* combined forces for a march past *en masse.* There's a lot to be said for and against bagpipes, but two hundred and fifty bandsmen at full throttle, on the march, kilts swinging, pipes skirling and drums rattling is a very impressive spectacle indeed.

Another impressive display was the march of the Lonach Highlanders, tough-looking warriors armed with claymores and pikes, led by banners and representing a piece of local history. After the Battle of Culloden in 1746 where the Highland army of Bonnie Prince Charlie, perhaps more properly called Charles Edward Stuart, was cut to pieces by the Duke of Cumberland's English troops, it was declared illegal to wear the kilt, symbol of Scottishness, and the penalty for being caught wearing the offending garment was death. Many Highlanders defied the edict and in disciplined groups marched over the hills, evading Cumberland's dragoons and keeping the hopes of the Stuart supporters alive. Today, of course, the only penalty for wearing the kilt is the possibility of getting chapped legs but the Lonach men keep the tradition of their forbears and as I heard an Australian visitor explain to another, 'they go walkabout' for the delectation of the crowds at Highland gatherings.

The actual site of the Gathering is a field of springy, close-cropped turf about the size of a small cricket (or baseball) ground, surrounded by stands (bleachers for the most part) and a flurry of tents for committee and competitors at one corner, always assuming that an oval can be said to have corners. The Royal Box or pavilion, heavily decorated with heather, rowan and the royal coat of arms, is so placed as to command a view of the proceedings and so arranged that the proceedings, or rather those engaged in them, can get a good view of the occupants of the Royal Box. To the right, as you face the Royal Box, are covered stands and to their right a towering, uncovered grandstand. The balance of the seats, or to be accurate benches, seem to have been donated by various organizations connected with the north-east of Scotland such as Drambuie the distillers, Amoco, Mobil (North Sea) Limited, Bristows Helicopters, Chubb Fire Security, and many others. By mid-morning all seats, sponsored or not, were full and in addition a huge crowd was standing on turf banks watching

144

the events or refreshing itself with hot dogs and fruit slices, being photographed with pipers in full regalia by relatives, chatting with complete strangers or meeting compatriots in the Overseas Visitors Tent.

Proceedings started at 10 am sharp and continued on schedule until the last weight had been thrown, the last jump had been made and the last bagpipe had wheezed into silence. Among the myriad sights and sounds of the Gathering, I noticed, as the massed bands were forming up, a diminutive drum major from Aberdeen Ladies Pipe Band being given a few hints on manipulation of the baton from her counterpart from another band, a vast man in scarlet uniform jacket and Stuart tartan kilt, both of them laughing and chatting, clearly enjoying the exchange and then watched them later poker-faced and in perfect time leading the parade.

An Austrian visitor in leather trousers and tyrolean hat, moving among the crowd, stared after by two Scots in full Highland regalia. One Scot saying to the other, 'Jamie, did ye notice yon wee foreigner in that outlandish costume?'

A bewildered Persian lady in the Overseas Visitors Tent trying to find Iran on a map of Australia and being directed to the right map by a courteous Japanese.

A pretty, blonde dancer preparing to compete in the sword dance limbering up with a sequence of leaps and springs as nimble and composed as a young Margot Fonteyn.

The bewildering number and variety of tartans each more eye-catching than the last — and the old joke flashing through my mind: 'Is there anything worn under the kilt?' 'No, madam. It's all in perfect working order.'

The surprise of learning that only since the sex equality act have women been allowed to compete in the games (although there were no female competitors tossing the caber I noticed, and as the Braemar caber is a tree trunk nineteen feet nine inches long and weighting 132 pounds, I'm not surprised). When I expressed the view that the kilt was the perfect unisex garment I was informed with a twinkle 'Och no — it's a man's clothing. The lasses who wear the kilts are really transvestites.'

The thing that stands out in your mind about the Braemar Gathering is its friendliness. The Scots are a hospitable folk who seem to want to share what they have with the visitor. I wouldn't say the Scots were a nation of chatterboxes but there's a lot in a smile and a nod and there's something about the atmosphere of a place that's genuinely friendly which communicates itself to you without words. Braemar is such a place.

The Gathering is very much a royal occasion, but it hasn't been got up *just* to amuse the monarch. The Gathering has been in existence in one form or another for a thousand years. It's a test of strength (if you can throw a twenty-eight pound stone over forty feet you're *strong*), grace (as anyone watching an expertly-danced reel will agree), speed (I watched a hundred-yard sprint won in 9.8 seconds), and independence (ninety per cent of the events are all against all, and the only team sports, the tug of war and the four by four-hundred yards relay, are provided by outsiders). These qualities are not unique to Scottish Highlanders — but they possess them all and it's a joy to spend even a brief few hours in their company.

When Winter Comes

First a question. Who said: 'The English Winter ends in July, to recommence in August'? Well, it was Lord Byron, but he was besotted by Greece at the time and, as the Billy Wilder film so succinctly puts it, 'Some like it hot'.

To be frank, it's no good coming to Britain in winter if your heart is set on sunkissed beaches and waving palms. Byron exaggerated, of course, but the winter on these shores lasts from November until March or thereabouts, and while the Scillies and the Channel Islands will be mild, and St Andrews in Scotland probably free of ice and snow in any quantity during these months, a visitor to our shores in the short months of the year needs — well — at least a raincoat.

What to do when 'Icicles hang by the wall and Dick the Shepherd blows his nail'? Well, there's skiing in Aviemore in Scotland, golf — weather permitting — everywhere in the British Isles, the National Cat Club Show at Olympia in December, a Chess Congress in Hastings in January, the International Boat Show at Earl's Court also in January, and masses of Rugby Union football.

Clearly, the kingpin of winter is Christmas, and though the Scots make a bigger celebration of Hogmanay, the English celebrate Christmas in a big way. In fact, since Dickens's day the holiday seems to have *stretched* and now occupies most of December, and lingers into January. Theatrical entertainments of all sorts boom at this time of the year, and in many towns and cities theatres which are 'dark' (that is to say, not functioning) during the rest of the year dust off the red plush, polish the brass and tune up the orchestra in preparation for the annual pantomime. If you have never seen an English pantomime let me describe it to you as it was once described to me by an awestruck American friend.

It was something else. There is this poor kid by the name of Cinderella who is being put down by these two old broads. Only they're not broads, right, they are guys. Can you beat that? Two guys dressed up as dolls giving the old ackamarackus to this little legit broad, Cinders. So anyway — then in comes this old guy dressed as a page boy with brass buttons all over his uniform, looking like a 1956 ad for Philip Morris cigarettes. He sees that Cinders is moping more than somewhat so he says, 'Hey why so glum?' or words to that effect, and they do a song and dance routine to 'Putting On The Ritz'. Now in comes Cinders's father who is an even older guy than the one in the button suit, and he enters into the spirit of the proceedings by going around and about and up and down saying how the family are flat busted and Cinders has to go out and collect what she describes as faggots but which turn out to be nothing but twigs.

So there she is in the forest, and there too is coming an old broad who is making out that life is plenty of 6 to 5 against, and Cinders gives the old broad the big hello and the faggots (that's to say twigs). Then the old doll straightens up and says like I'm your fairy godmother and whatsoever you shall want be sure it'll be a boat race and you'll be swimming in mink and champagne if you say the word. Well, by now what with the transvestites and faggots and fairies I'm wondering 'whatever next', but now comes one or two dames dressed as guys but in the States no guys could go out like that without getting arrested, except perhaps in San Francisco.

These two rap back and forth about one being the Prince and the other his servant, Dandini. Hey, why don't they change roles – and I figure everything else is changed — the hell with it, why not? And they do and the Prince gets to meet Cinderella and there's a ball and a slipper and mice and pumpkins and a search and all ends happily for one and all, but I'm left figuring how is Cinders going to put together a stable emotional relationship when she's the only one who

148

plays it right down the line — sex-wise — in the whole enterprise?

Alternative Christmas Messages

One of the absolute certainties of journalism is that when Christmas approaches editors start to fidget and long discussions are held to decide how Christmas should be tackled by the various magazines and newspapers. My contribution to a Christmas Number one year was a series of blueprints for 'alternative' Christmas messages, to be presented on television on Christmas Day by an assortment of minority groups.

The first Christmas message comes from the Secretary of the National Association Of Unisex Transvestite Zen Better Life Through Eating Nature's Way And Ratepayers Society.

We are a loosely-knit federation whose mutual interests have come together on a basis of the free association of compatible inter-related groups whose interests are mutually compatible to the joint aims of our loosely-knit federation. It is early days yet, and not unlike the beginnings of the Nazi party but without the uniforms, or the racialist sexist overtones or the inhibiting and rigid nationalism, or indeed invading Poland. I have been asked to make this Yuletide address to the nation as it was felt that from the transvestite point of view we have not had the exposure we have every right (in view of our numbers and voting power) to expect. As a vegetarian ratepayer, I can claim further rights within our loosely-knit federation and what's more, I look more like the Queen than the others — apart from the moustache and glasses. Admittedly, a moustache on a transvestite and spectacles on a health food addict are not, on the face of it, a good advertisement for our cause, but we in our group feel that my appearance will reinforce the points of view held by the ratepaying wing of our loosely-knit federation.

The unisex splinter group are more than catered for in this address by the fact that I am a working mother with two wee ones at the local Buddhist kindergarten, and a hubby who is a male stripper.

In this time of traditional peace and tranquillity, we of the National Association of Unisex Transvestite Zen Better Life Through Eating Nature's Way And Ratepayers Society, are proud to look back on a year when we have made a profound impact on society as a whole.

149

Two new branches have been opened, one in Billericay and one in Wick, bringing the total to three, and our membership has soared into double figures.

On behalf of us all, may I wish you whether transvestites, frond fans, exponents of the unisex view, zen enthusiasts, or ratepayers — Godspeed, and a tranquil New Year.

The next alternative Queen's Speech is on behalf of Anglo Afghan Import/Export Free Expression And Nirvana Club.

Hey, man, like, is it Christmas Day? Oh — isn't it beautiful? I mean, it's beautiful. Look...look...hey, man, look at *that*, that's beautiful but really you know, beautiful. It's too *much* you know that? Hey... oh, hey...oh...hey...oh...You know what? Life is terrific and...and, and will you look at that? That's beautiful. I want to tell you something that will blow your mind. It's like the real thing. Listen...it seems to have slipped my mind, but what the hell — it's a beautiful day, so be beautiful...be beautiful. Be — be-au-ti-ful.

Captain Wanscott-Harpenden speaks for the Society For The Protection Of The Indigenous Population Of This Sceptred Isle.

Good afternoon. Compliments of the season. My good lady and I were horrified when we returned to the old country, after a lifetime in rubber, to find the many changes that had overtaken our beloved land. Our Society, which is growing daily, is pledged under God and the Queen (two pretty good patrons, I think you'll agree) to put this blessed sod back on to an even keel. When I see the streets of what was formerly the greatest Capital city in the world thronged with blackamoors driving boch, wop and nipponese motor cars, paid for, I have no doubt, by National Assistance, I feel frankly sick. I am no stranger to wogs of all types, and their dissipated and unhygienic mode of life, sleeping often twenty to a room, roaming the streets, mugging elderly white people, and fermenting strikes.

I am told that unemployment in Great Britain is approximately 4 million. The solution is therefore simple. Send 4 million of these people back where they came from. By doing this we would immediately secure three advantages: 1) our unemployment figures would be cut, at a stroke, to nil; 2) The indigenous population of these islands could once again walk the streets at night without fear of molestation; and 3) (if I may be allowed to jest at this festive season) there'd be two hours more daylight in Brixton.

Until that day comes, as assuredly it will, we shall continue to press on with the formation of local defence groups to patrol the streets suitably equipped to deal with hooligans, using methods perfected by our good friends in the more salubrious parts of South Africa. So, woe betide any member of the disease-ridden alien hordes who takes the law into his own hands.

Let me say, in conclusion, and I know I'm supported by the majority of right-thinking Britishers, that in twelve months time in this great land of ours, we shall be celebrating a truly white Christmas.

I thank you.

And now Christmas from the point of view of the Walthamstow Badger Club.

My badger and I greet you this cheery Christmastide, and to badger lovers everywhere we say — How long must we suffer under the lash of public indifference at this season of goodwill to all men and badgers. My word, we've seen some ups and downs, what with the drought and everything, and there's one thing that's always puzzled me, why on the BBC weather forecasts don't you ever see what the weather's like in Eire. They must have weather it stands to reason, but you don't see so much as an isobar on the weather map. It's a puzzle all right, like the National Assistance, which is called something else nowadays. That's a word Oscar Wilde used a lot in his plays, 'nowadays', but that's not to suggest I, that is, my badger and I, have anything in common with O. Wilde, but he was Irish so perhaps there is a cosmic pattern that includes us all irrespective of sex, race or creed. Ditto O. Henry, albeit a fish of a different complexion. Oh, now I remember, it's called Social Security — and unemployment offices are called job centres, and it's the same with badgers. Lipservice but in reality cynical indifference. Badgers are harmless and do good so let me give you this message. Help a badger find his feet and you'll have made a loyal and true friend. Goodbye.

Finally and briefly, here is the Christmas message from the League For Democratic Non-Partisan Law Enforcement.

Hello. Our Christmas message is this — Stuff the fuzz. I thank you.

Quiz: Oneupmanship

And to while away the rest of Christmas — a Oneupmanship quiz.

Oneupmanship, the invention of Stephen Potter, can be defined as 'The art of going one better than your fellows in spite of being naturally inferior'.

The quiz is based on this philosophy. Why don't you try it and discover your own upmanship quotient (your UQ INDEX).

Section A. Healthmanship

If you're a doctor it is the art of getting one up on your patient without actually killing him. If you're a patient it is the art of discomfiting the doctor.

(For Patients Only)

1. Is it better to be
   - a) Healthy at all times.
   - b) Constantly ill.
   - c) A mixture of both.

2. A good Lifeman will develop an interesting and bogus affliction. In order of merit which rates higher
   - a) The imperious stammer.
   - b) The attention inviting tremor.
   - c) The romantic limp.

3. When visiting a Harley Street Specialist should the patient
   - a) Talk about friends in high places (e.g. Buckingham Palace).
   - b) Discuss the merits of a rival Specialist two doors up the street.
   - c) Describe in detail acupuncture.

4. When seeing a General Practitioner for the first time should you
   - a) Describe your symptoms in detail.
   - b) Undress immediately.
   - c) Bet the doctor a pound he can't guess what you've got.

5. If you want to unsettle your doctor — who has the highest irritant value

a) Dr Spock.
b) Albert Schweitzer.
c) The Minister of Health.

(For Doctors Only)
6. Should the doctor tell the nervous patient that

a) He's worrying too much.
b) He's worrying too little.
c) Twenty-five years ago he'd have been dead.

7. All doctors have a number of large and impressive volumes in their consulting rooms. The doctor who practises Lifemanship should consult

a) Ruff's *Guide To The Turf*.
b) A manual of Veterinary Surgery.
c) The *Dog Lover's Companion*.

8. When on house calls, which has a higher patient upping rating

a) a 1983 Porsche.
b) A 1938 Bentley.
c) A bicycle.

Section B. Businessmanship
Stephen Potter offers the equation Businessmanship = Salesmanship = Lifemanship. How good a businessman/woman are you?

9. Is your best approach to your client one of

a) Complete self assurance.
b) Total indifference.
c) Utter incompetence.

153

10. When signing contracts
should you use

    a) A gold-topped fountain pen
with your initials on it.
b) A Japanese felt-tipped pen.
c) Have no pen at all and
borrow the other chap's.

11. Which of the following
perfumes should your
secretary wear

    a) Arpège.
b) Chanel No. 5.
c) Ma Griffe.

(NB — If you have a male secretary do not answer this question)

Section C. Woomanship
Based on Stephen Potter's *Guide to Courtship*

12. On meeting a pretty girl for
the first time at a party
should you

    a) Offer to get her into
showbusiness.
b) Applaud her common sense
for not being in
showbusiness.
c) Offer to marry her.

13. Flowers play an important
part in wooing. In the
language of flowers what do
the following stand for

    a) A deep red carnation.
b) Everflowering candytuft.
c) A pineapple.

14. The true Lifewoman can, of course, choose to marry any man she wishes. Place in order of desirability the following

   a) 23-year-old six-foot tall Swiss skiing instructor.
   b) 35-year-old medium size warehouseman.
   c) 79-year-old millionaire.

15. If you're a man, is it better to be

   a) Handsome.
   b) Ugly.
   c) Rich.

16. All the world loves a lover. Complete the following pairs

   a) Dante and
   b) Tristan and
   c) Fortnum and

Section D. Weekendmanship
17. You are invited by rich friends to stay with them in the country for the weekend. Should you travel

   a) By car.
   b) By rail.
   c) In your host's helicopter.

18. If while playing Bridge you and your partner are being soundly beaten should you

   a) Complain about your luck.
   b) Accept defeat gracefully.
   c) Start using marked cards.

19. On the grouse moor the Gamesman has many options. Should he

   a) Shoot everything in sight.
   b) Use blank cartridges.
   c) Bird watch.

Section E. Artsmanship

20. The object of the Lifeman in matters of the Arts is to take the counter of philistine point of view. In this context place in their incorrect or 'games' order the following
    a) Fragonard.
    b) Andy Warhol.
    c) Ford Maddox Brown.

21. At the theatre should the Gamesman
    a) Hiss angrily at latecomers.
    b) Eat crisps throughout the play.
    c) Stay in the bar.

22. To the student of Lifemanship the study of Music is not important but in which order would you place these musical instruments for their irritant effect
    a) The trombone.
    b) The cor anglais.
    c) The flute.

Section F. Golfmanship

'The games game of games games' is how Stephen Potter describes golf, a sport in which the Gamesman can truly come into his own.

23. Your opponent is 2 up at the 9th. Which phrase is most likely to disconcert him
    a) Take it easy, it's only a game.
    b) I shall have more time for golf now that I've been made redundant.
    c) The doctor says this is the last game I shall ever be able to play.

That's the quiz. Here are the answers as approved by the Stephen Potter Institute of Oneupmanship, Yeovil.

1. a = 5   b = 5   c = 0
2. a = 3   b = 5   c = 2
3. a = 3   b = 3   c = 3
4. a = 0   b = 4   c = 5
5. a = 0   b = 0   c = 5
6. a = 4   b = 4   c = 3
7. a = 3   b = 5   c = 4
8. a = 2   b = 3   c = 0
9. a = 0   b = 2   c = 5
10. a = 0   b = 3   c = 5
11. a = 5   b = 5   c = 5
12. a = 0   b = 2   c = 0

13. a) Alas for my poor heart.
    b) Indifference.
    c) You are perfect.
    Score 5 for each correct answer.

14. The correct order is, of course, c, a, b.
    Score 5 for this, otherwise 0.

15. a = 2   b = 2   c = 5

16. a) Beatrice.
    b) Isolde.
    c) Mason.
    Score 5 for each correct answer.

17. a = 0   b = 0   c = 0
    The correct answer is — In your *own* helicopter.
    Score 10 for this.

18. a = 5*   b = 0   c = 0
    (NB* Gamesmanship is the art of winning games without actually cheating)

19. a = 5   b = 5   c = 5

20. This is a trick question to which there is no answer.

21. a = 0   b = 4   c = 5

22. a = 4   b = 3   c = 5*
    (*If you don't believe me you have never heard Richard
    Briers struggling with the flute!)

23. a = 3   b = 4   c = 5

The possible score is 135.

If you have scored 110–135 you are in the top bracket of
Oneupmen. (If you looked at the answers first you're disqualified.
See note on answer to question 18.)

If you scored 60–100 you are a good all round Gamesman and
should do well in politics.

If you scored 15–60 you must try harder.

If you scored 0–15 you are naive, gullible or thick and I'd be
delighted to sell you a second-hand car.

This book reuses some material previously published elsewhere. It is based on:

Part 1: Views

'Forced to Tour' *In Britain* October 1974
'Anything to Get Into Show Business' *Punch* March 1974
'Escape' *Punch* January 1974
'Small Top' *Punch* September 1974
'Great Days' *Punch* September 1974 and December 1975
'2L.O. to Goodbye from him' *Television Today* June 1980
'Going Commercial' *Television Today* September 1976
'TV or no TV...?' *Punch* June 1978
'Love That Soap' *Daily Mail* October 1980
'The Identikit Soap Opera' *Daily Mail* February 1977
'History of the World So Far' *Daily Mail* November 1979
'Tony Hancock: Genius (Failed)' *Radio Times* October 1978
'The Sublime Peter Sellers' *Punch* July 1978
'Woody and Annie' *Punch* October 1977
'Obit I — Groucho' *Punch* September 1977
'Obit II — Charlie Chaplin' *Punch* January 1978
'Dick and Ian Porridge' *Radio Times* July 1974
'Susan Harris — The Woman Behind Soap' *Daily Mail* March 1980
'Alan Whicker' *Daily Mail* November 1978
'Raymond Briggs' *The Bookseller*
'Overheard at the Club' *Advertising Agency*

Part 2: Reviews

'There Aint Nobody Here But Us Chicks' *Punch* August 1977
'John, Paul, George, Ringo — and Bert' *Punch* August 1974
'A Hat Full of Musicals' *Punch* July 1980
'Hello Carol — Goodbye Dolly' *Punch* September 1979
'Waiting for Colin' *Punch* July 1975
'Farce From my Elbow — The Old Vic' *Punch* October 1976
'A.H. and Noises Off' *Punch* March 1982
'The Mousetrap' *In Britain* November 1976
'Films' (pp 87–90) *Punch* December 1977
'How Not To Write A Film Script' *White Elephant House Magazine* 1975
'The American Way' *Punch* January 1978
'Me And The Movies' *Punch* September 1977
'Mixed Bag' *Punch* February 1979
'That Was The Year That Was' *Punch* December 1978
'Watch this Space' *Punch* March 1978
'The Dancing Chicken' *Punch* January 1978
'Awfully Bloody — Bloody Awful' *Punch* June 1978
'Strange Doings' *Punch* October 1978
'Not Angels But Choirboys' *Punch* February 1978
'Mad About Ludwig' *Punch* October 1978
'Who Swallowed the Formula?' *Punch* February 1979
'The First Deadly Sin' *Daily Mail* May 1981
'The Fan' *Daily Mail* May 1981

'Nighthawks' *Daily Mail* June 1981
'Post-Post-Script' *Punch* June 1978

Part 3: Reflections

'Oh to be in England' *In Britain* Spring 1981
'Excuse me, Which one is the Queen?' *In Britain* June 1978
'Sumer is i-cumen in' *In Britain* Summer 1982
'Son Of The Beach' *High Life* May 1978
'Cannes Do' *Punch* June 1978
'Those Autumn Leaves' *In Britain* Spring 1982
'The Braemar Gathering' *In Britain* September 1977
'When the Winter Comes…' *In Britain* Winter 1982
'Alternative Christmas Messages' *Punch* December 1976
'Quiz: oneupmanship' *Radio Times* February 1976